Marx right side up – Capitalism, Class Struggle, and the Recovery of Marx's Project

By Sarah Philipson, Associate Professor Emerita

ISBN 978-91-531-7973-3

Revised 2nd edition

Philipson Publishing

Content

Abstract

For Marx and Engels, the workers' liberation must be their own achievement. To do that, the forces of production must evolve to the extent that workers' experience and scientific knowledge enable them to manage production by themselves.

All hitherto so-called socialist and communist revolutions has been carried out by self-appointed so-called workers' representatives that have acquired dictatorial power by promising to 'give' the workers their liberation, which has never happened.

Capitalism does not in itself develop the productive forces to the necessary extent; the workers must force capitalism to do so; thus, gaining influence over the work process through class struggle.

This article shows how such influence can be achieved by studying the influence gained by creating a workers' council at the Korsnäs paper mill in Sweden in the 1980s and 1990s. It is thus possible; the question is how this can be generalized and sustained over time.[1]

---

1 The figures in Chapters 2–4 are analytical abstractions, not empirical descriptions of firms

Keywords

forces of production; workers' councils; workers' influence; fighting alienation; class struggle; strata of classes; Newspeak (Orwell, 1949)

1. Introduction – Framing the Problem

The unfruitful and un-dialectical polemic between the second and third international, whether reform ***or*** revolution was the right path to socialism, delivered neoliberalism as the result of the reform strategy and "red" dictatorship as a result of the revolutionary strategy; both far from the socialism envisaged by Marx and Engels.

In the communist manifesto, Marx and Engels promised a better world, but history has not delivered that; at least so far. Marx conceived communism as a vision of social liberty and human fulfillment. History has so far tainted his visions with the history of dictatorships and instances of genocide that have been justified through interpretations that, as this book shows, are not based on Marx. So-called socialist countries, such as the Soviet Union, China, Cambodia, and North Korea, has committed atrocities in the name of Marx' vision. Are these necessary consequences of his vision? Or could Marxism be revitalized to fulfill promises?

Marxist economics has seen the capitalist economy as not only determining, but deterministic to evolution. But the capitalist economy is determining the evolution of the capitalist ***society*** only as long as the class struggle does not ***transcend*** the capitalist society.[2] As the class struggle is limited by this economy, such a transcendence, called a revolution, can only be achieved if the working class fights the capitalist subsumption of the work process under capitalism.

We will show that the hitherto socialist revolutions were not based on such an understanding, at least in ***practice***, although not necessarily in ***theory***[3], of how such a transcendence could be achieved according to Marx and Engels[4].

This book aims to answer why Marxism has so far failed to fulfill its promises and what is required to achieve such a fulfillment, by studying what caused the failures, what is needed in the form of developing the experience, learning, and capabilities for workers' liberation and what the conditions are to achieve these.

---

[2] Marx and Engels were adamant that *"The history of all hitherto existing society is the history of class struggles."* (Marx and Engels, 1848:14).

[3] *"Only struggle educates the exploited class. Only struggle discloses to it the magnitude of its own power, widens its horizon, enhances its abilities, clarifies its mind, forges its will."* (Lenin 1917: 241, cited after Wolfson, & Funke, 2018: 577). While, as I will show, his practice was the opposite to this statement.

[4] Marx and Engels were clear that *"... the working class cannot simply lay hold of ready-made state machinery, and wield it for its own purposes."* (Marx, & Engels, 1948: 9).

The failure of Marxism has not been primarily theoretical, but practical: it misunderstood the conditions under which workers can acquire the capabilities to govern production.

This book therefore asks whether, and under what competitive and institutional conditions, workers can acquire real influence over production within capitalism itself – and whether such experiences can accumulate into a material basis for transition.

How to read this book

This book is not organized as a linear exposition of a single theory, nor as a chronological history. It is structured as a progressive reconstruction of Marx's project, moving across different analytical levels and returning repeatedly to the same core problem from new angles.

Early chapters develop the systemic logic of capitalism, emphasizing uneven subsumption, differentiated capital functions, and the coexistence of distinct competitive regimes. These chapters should be read as establishing analytical distinctions rather than advancing political conclusions.

Middle chapters shift the focus to class structure, institutions, and learning, introducing capability formation, tacit knowing, and workers' influence over production as material processes. Here, empirical and theoretical arguments are deliberately interwoven. The Korsnäs case should not be read as an example to be generalized mechanically, but as a demonstration of how specific historical conditions make certain forms of class struggle possible – and fragile.

Later chapters synthesize these strands into a theory of transition. Transition is treated neither as an event nor as an automatic outcome of crisis, but as a temporally extended process in which institutions, competition, and learning interact. Political conclusions are therefore intentionally delayed until the necessary analytical groundwork has been laid.

Each chapter ends with a short systemic summary. These summaries are not substitutes for the chapters themselves, but guides to their internal logic. Readers interested primarily in the overall argument may read the summaries first and return selectively to the chapters; readers interested in theory-building are encouraged to read the book sequentially.

All figures, diagrams, and tables are the author's own, unless otherwise explicitly stated.

The book is written against economistic, mechanical, and authoritarian interpretations of Marx, but it does not proceed polemically. Disagreements emerge through analysis rather than denunciation. Readers are invited to engage critically with the argument, rather than treating individual chapters as stand-alone positions.

2. Capitalism as a System – Marx Theory of Capitalism

The purpose of this chapter is not to restate Marx for exegetical reasons, but to reconstruct those elements of his theory that are necessary to understand (a) why capitalism does not automatically generate the capacities required for its transcendence, and (b) why class struggle must therefore take the form of a struggle over the subsumption of capital functions. Competition here is not a market abstraction, but a coercive social relation operating through capital mobility.

The chapter proceeds by visual abstraction. The figures are not pedagogical aids, but analytical models, intended to make visible relations that are obscured in purely textual exposition.

2.1 Capitalism as a competitive system

Central to the vision of Marx and Engels in the Communist Manifesto was that the working class was uniquely situated to transform the present capitalist society to a classless society and liberate humanity. But also, that this transformation (they used the word revolution to signify the extent of such a transformation) must the working class's own work. (Marx, & Engels, 1848: 62).

2.2 Subsumption

In this book, subsumption refers to the process by which human activities, institutions, and social relations are progressively reorganized under the logic of capital. This is not limited to the direct control of labour in production, but extends to the ways in which practices, expectations, and forms of cooperation are shaped and stabilized through economic and institutional arrangements.

Subsumption is therefore not a one-time transformation, but an ongoing process through which the conditions of social reproduction are aligned with the requirements of capital accumulation.

Internal relations of production – formal and real subsumption

The only Marxists who have bothered with Marx's concepts of productive forces and subsumption are Bettelheim and Braverman. Bettelheim succeeds in a concrete analysis of the transition between feudalism and capitalism (Bettelheim, 1970a, 1976), but fails when he attempts a corresponding analysis of the transition between capitalism and socialism (Bettelheim, 1970a, 1970b, 1970c, 1970d, 1971a, 1971b, 1972, 1973; Bettelheim, Charriere, & Marchisio, 1968). Braverman (1977) clearly shows the subordination of the working class under capitalism, but makes the mistake of thinking that the working class must ***necessarily*** become increasingly subordinate under capitalism. Instead, I hold that it is necessary to ***struggle*** to try to impose the workers' own subsumption of the capital functions, within capitalism; to "eat up" capitalism from within, in the same way that capitalism blew up feudalism through the publishing system and the mills.

External conditions of production – The market

Classical economics, especially Ricardo and Marx, were micro-economists. They showed how the competition between individual enterprises and the social relations created by and within these, created the capitalist system with its inherent tendencies. It spread nationally and globally a capitalist society, with a capitalist production system and simple commodity production, and remnants of various previous systems. This contrasts with neoclassical economists, who believe that capitalism is limited by a macro-market. Granovetter's (1985) criticism of the later Nobel laureate Williamsson (1973, 1992) for his inability to understand that the market is ***embedded*** in social relations, was based on classical economics.

2.3 The capitalist process of production

In the capitalist production process, raw materials are taken in and processed by workers using machines to produce goods that are sold in a market. To operate the machines, energy (electricity, water, steam, etc.) and other necessities (lubricating oils, etc.) are required.

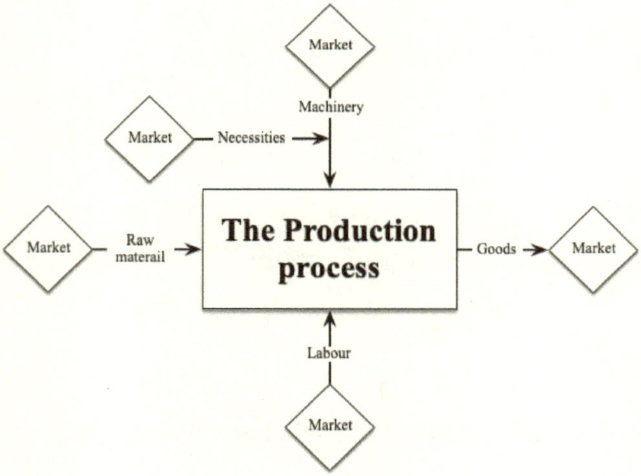

Figure 1. Capitalist production.

Marx showed the dual nature of this process, its material physical and its economic. manifestation.

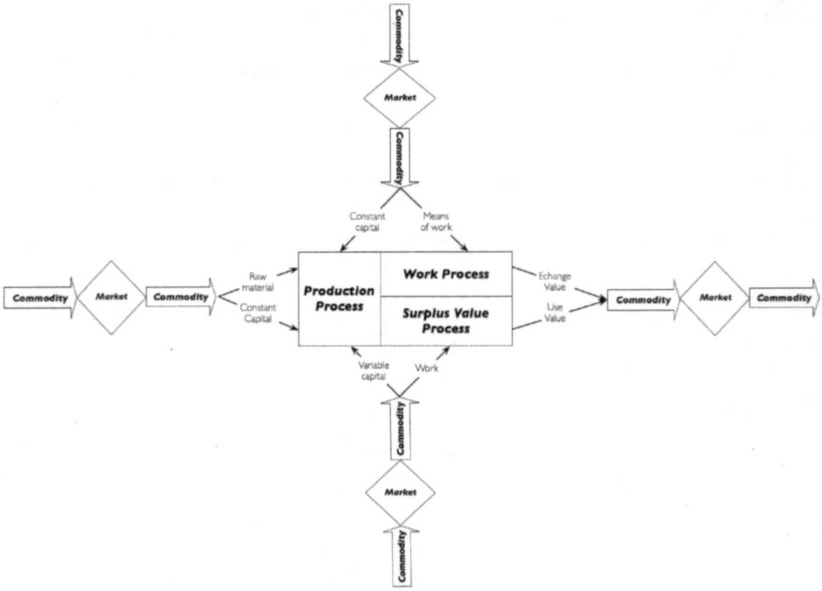

Figure 2. The two aspects of capitalist production, as labor process and as profit-making process.

The Capitalist production process is characterized by capital being used to produce an exchange value, what a buyer is prepared and has the resources to pay for a product or service. For it to be meaningful to the capitalist, this exchange value must be greater than the resources needed to produce the exchange value. The difference is called surplus value.

The resources that the capitalist invests in the production process on an ongoing basis (costs in modern business economics) can be divided into three types:

1. ***Fixed constant capital***, the wear and tear (depreciation) of machinery, buildings and other equipment needed.
2. The resources used to purchase raw materials and semi-finished products needed, ***variable constant capita***l.
3. The wages paid to the productive workers to dispose of their working capacity for a certain time, ***variable capital***.

The asymmetric transaction

Use value for the buyer, exchange value for the seller.

The seller is more interested in the value of the money the seller receives for his product more than the value of this product.

The buyer is more interested in the value of the item more than the money the buyer pays for the item.

Organic composition

Organic composition is a measure of how advanced the capital is. It is the share of the fixed constant capital in the total capital. The more automated the production, the greater the profit that can be produced per working hour.

Added value

All use-value is created through human labor and raw materials from nature. The exchange value is the socially necessary labor time to produce a product or service. How then can the capitalist realize a profit, a surplus value, beyond the use values for which he has paid? The use-value of labor – the working time – which the capitalist buys for the worker's exchange value (the cost of reproducing, recreating, the commodity labor-power), the wage – produces this surplus value. In the capitalist system of production and its necessary legal structure, where the wage is the correct price for labor time, the sale of labor power is not forced upon the worker; therefore, the worker is not 'cheated' by the capitalist.

The wage is only problematic from a moral and therefore political perspective; not an economic or legal one.

2.4 Capitalist production as a whole

Marx distinguished two main "departments" in capitalist production, Department I which manufactures raw materials and means of production (machines, factories, office buildings, etc.).

The production of raw materials and the production of means of production are separated in figure 3 below. These are inputs to Department I itself and to Department II. Department II manufactures goods for consumption, consumer goods industry. Reproduction is the re-creation of labor (food, education, healthcare, etc.). In Figure 3, reproduction is divided into the reproduction of the workers who work in raw material production, the production of means of production, and those who work in the consumer goods industry.

1. ***Department I***, companies that manufacture means of production. Within Department I, the following industries are distinguished:
    1. Extraction of raw materials and
    2. Manufacturing machines and other equipment for capitalist production,
    3. Manufacture of munitions.
2. ***Department II***, companies producing consumer goods, i.e. goods used in reproduction.
3. ***Reproduction***, family, school, university, care of the sick and old. Reproduction takes place outside the capitalist system of production, *except to the extent that Department II firms produce services for reproduction*[5]. A distinction is made between three subgroups:
    - a). the state: police, military, civil servants.
    - b). reproduction of unproductive workers.
    - c). reproduction of productive workers.

---

[5] See the discussion under Chapter 5. Classes and strata, below.

Productive workers work in Department I and II. The fact that those who work in reproduction are not productive does not mean that they are not necessary. Productive and unproductive labor is not a moral question, but a question of the extent to which they are productive in relation to the capitalist's production of surplus value.

Figure 3 shows A. Raw material extraction, B. Production of means of production, C. Production of means of reproduction, D. Reproduction of productive workers, E. Unproductive sector, and F. Reproduction of unproductive workers. The left-hand side represents Departments I and II as systemically structured in Marx’s analysis in Capital Volumes I–III, where relations are organized as discrete, one-directional sequences.

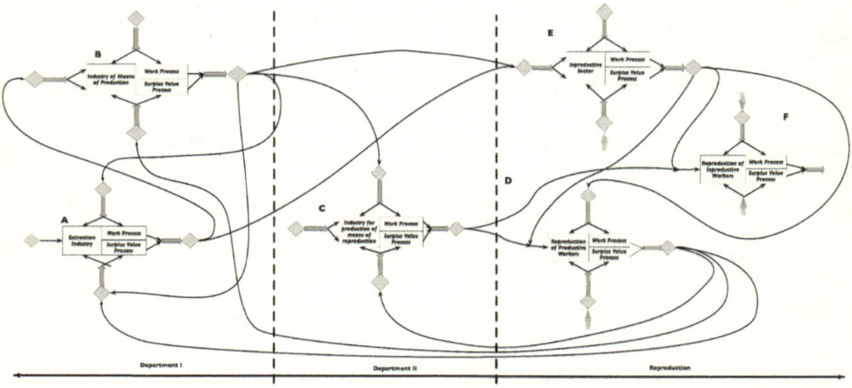

Figure 3. Sections I and II and the reproduction.

The right-hand side represents the process of reproduction. While it is conditioned by Department II, it is not governed by the same strictly economic terms but unfolds as an open set of interdependent relations that are only partially subsumed under the logic of capital.

2.5 Product structure, virtual product structure, and function structure

How production is done is not without consequences. Because capitalist production is internally differentiated into functions and product architectures, competition does not necessarily operate uniformly across the firm or the value chain. The implications of this structural differentiation for price-based and value-based competition is developed in Chapter 4. Parts of the analysis in Sections 2.5 and Chapter 3 are based on, but substantially revised and extended arguments, first developed in Philipson (2022b), originally published in ***International Journal of Innovation and Technology Management*** (World Scientific).

Product structure[6]

When the medieval carpenter produced a table, he didn't need a plan; everything was in his head, based on years of experience. But in modern industry, labor is divided between many workers

[6] Philipson (2022b)

and the products are often more complex, and it is necessary to plan how e.g. the different pieces of a machine are going to be produced and assembled. The production of a simple offering is done with the logic of a product structure, where individual materials and simple work operations are gradually assembled to components and the final offering (from at the bottom to the finished product at the top in Fig. 4). The specification of the product structure is done by the physical characteristics of organizing its manufacture.

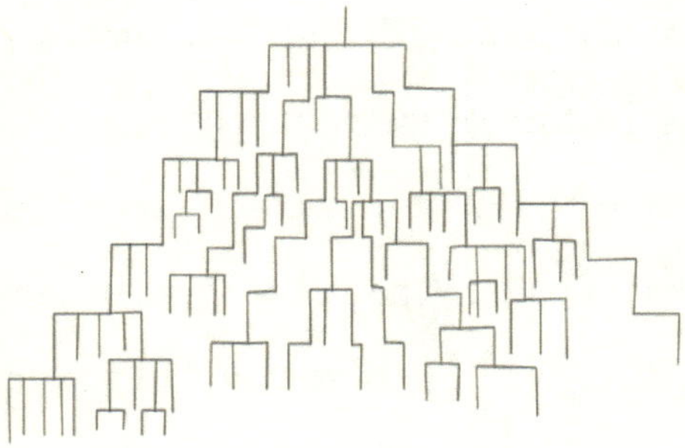

Figure 4. Simple product structure.

Virtual product structure, product platforms

Early in industrialization, products where usually produced as standard or special products. The most common, standard products, where produced for a market, many buyers, while the special products were the modern version of the medieval artisan, the production of a single machine, typically by a small engineering firm for a big manufacturing company.

But on small markets, as in the Scandinavian countries, it was difficult to get enough customers to produce standard products, and to produce special products was not cost-effective. Companies then developed standard-special products, where different components could be combined to several different end-products. It was less cost-effective than standard products, but more cost-effective than special products. Most academic literature thought that such standard-special manufacturing was the innovation of Japanese firms, as Japan was main competitor of the US.

The production of such standard-special products is represented by virtual product structures, where the finished product is the result of several engineering decisions (represented by the dashed lines in figure 5).

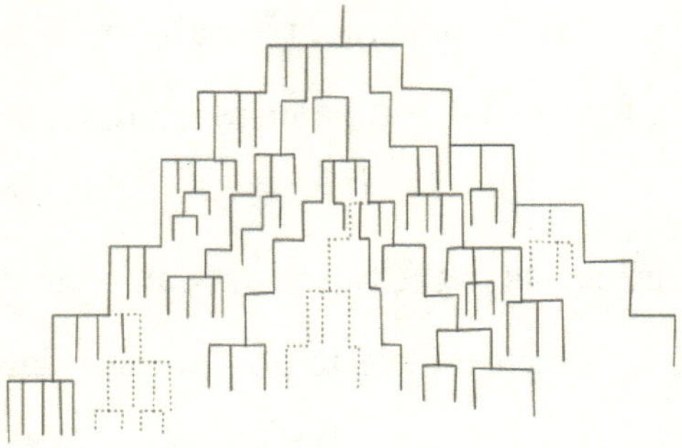

Figure 5. Virtual product structure.

A problem with standard-special products is that they involve a certain element of client-specific engineering, which delays giving a quote to the customer. To reduce the time to market for such standard-special products it is necessary automatize such client-specific engineering. 1990 I designed a computer-based quoting system with built-in engineering for a ABB filial, making it possible to immediately give quotes in 80-90% of the cases, as opposed to 20% before.

Increased competition forced companies to choose to offer standard-special products and/or to internationalize their operations, to find large enough markets.

Traditional outsourcing

Already in the 1950s, companies found that certain simple elements could be bought in the market, rather than manufactured in-house. Whole components could be outsourced to gain cost-effectiveness. This was for example typical in the car industry in the 1960s and 1970s. Already when companies made the decision to buy from the outside it was important to decide what parts of the product to outsource. The company needed to control tightly those elements of the product that was unique selling points, USPs, so that these features did not became available in the world market and hence accessible for competitors. They had to be produced in-house or, if the company did not have the necessary capabilities, with strategic partners, which in return for something for them strategically important, withheld the component from the world market; at least during a certain time.

Other components, while needing to have a sufficient quality to comply with other parts of the product, were considered to be non-selling points, NSPs (product functions considered to nonessential for competition), or matching points, MPs (product functions considered to reach a threshold in order for the product to be competitive). These could be bought at the lowest price on the world market, in order to facilitate the trade-off between USPs, MPs, and NSPs.

The firm had to design the outsourced component in every detail. To get quotes it must transfer all the necessary knowledge for its production, and the quotes must be analyzed in the same detail. This heavy load of knowledge transfer between buyer and seller limits the number of suppliers the firm can invite to give quotes. As a consequence, the price difference between the quotes is limited.

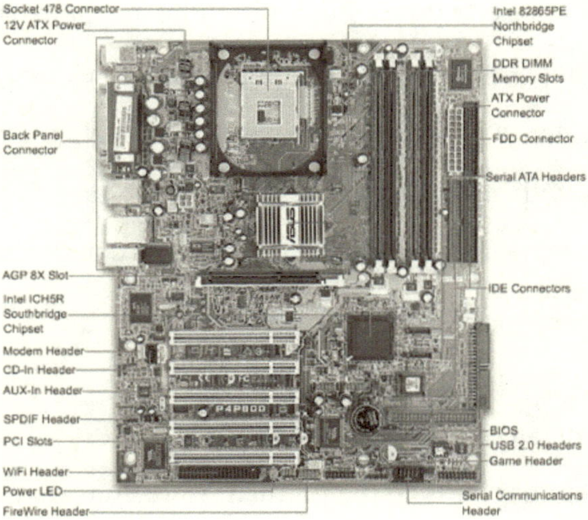

Figure 6. To the supplier/outsourcing, specifying in every detail.

The advantage that could be gained was mostly limited, because of (1) the cost of design, (2) transfer of information to the supplier, (3) evaluation of quotes, and (4) marginal difference between the quotes (as everything was a "given" by the buyer).

Wintelism[7]

In an anti-trust decision in 1980, IBM was forced to outsource its component manufacturing. The anti-trust authority hoped to create competition in the monopolized business machine market. IBM created a new way of outsourcing, based on just describing the ***functionality*** of the component and certain quality characteristics. Functionality is any attribute of the product from which the user derives a benefit, or what in economy is called a value. This became a global revolution; the emergence of a new form of outsourcing, often called Wintelism, permitted outsourcing to be made in a function structure (Ulrich, 1995:421), where individual functions of the offering, within a product architecture and specified interfaces between functions, were outsourced, with few specifications of how the physical components should realize the function. Wintelism revolutionized not only outsourcing, but also the world. It is the probably most important factor explaining the globalization in the last 40 years (Philipson, 2020b; 2022b).

Wintelism revolutionized not only outsourcing, but the world. It not only limited IBMs design work to the product architecture

---

[7] Studies concerning wintelism are limited in most western journals (see however Zysman, & Schwartz, 1998; Hart, & Kim, 2002; Tan, 2002; Kim, 2002; Lüthje, 2002; Bach, Newman, & Weber, 2005), but literally several hundred articles are published in Chinese journals (found by Google Scholar). However, all locked under password and in Chinese.

(the products as described by the functions of components); only limited information needed to be transferred to the potential supplier (later it could be published on a website and reach thousands of suppliers all over the world), it required limited information to evaluate the quotes from the suppliers, and often giving radical differences in price, because the suppliers could compete by developing new ways of manufacturing the component. The functional specification of the product architecture also facilitated innovation of the product, the value it was supposed to deliver the customer. The combined effects of innovation in architecture and components led to "Moore's law": the price of components either halved in 18 months or its capacity doubled. This led to a 2.300.000 times productivity increase in the electronics industry between 1980 and 2015 (Wikipedia, 2021-02-01). But even more important is that it is the probably most important factor explaining the globalization the last 50 years.

The flip side of these advantages are that capitalism has become more volatile (or risky), as more and more costs are becoming fixed (development of product architecture, organizing the supply-chain, investment in development of software and other intangible parts of the product, marketing), rather than variable costs, for producing each individual product. This combined with shortening life cycles of new products means that the lion's share of costs has to be taken before any product is sold (Philipson, 2021). They need to be paid upfront, before any product is sold. And the "window" to recuperate these costs and gain profit becomes shorter. The potential benefits spur companies to take these risks.

Less design work, faster design

Consequently, the buying firm don't need to "design" (innovate, product develop, construct) every detail of a product, only the " product architecture" on a "high" level of the product structure. This makes it is possible to develop in shorter time, which is very important with shorter and shorter product life cycles.

Increased competition among suppliers

Since the firm only must specify the function of the component (input – output), it is possible to transfer the information simple and inexpensively, e.g. by a web page, to many more suppliers, increasing the competition among suppliers. Often thousands of suppliers, rather than as before maybe some ten, can be invited. It also becomes less expensive to evaluate the offerings of the suppliers. And the firm don't need to transfer detailed knowledge to the supplier that has gained the bid – the supplier knows best how the component shall be produced.

The unleashing of creativity

The prospective suppliers can use their creativity to invent radically new solutions that either give much lower price, higher performance, or new features. Cf. the development in the computer industry since 1980.

Figure 7. Wintelism.

Standardization and innovation

What is the role of standardization in increasing innovation? Why does it have such an impact?

With the emerging of wintelism (Borrus, & Zysman, 1997; Hart, & Kim, 2002; Kim, 2002; Philipson, 2020b; Tan, 2002; Tsai, & Wright, 2014) in the early 1980s, it was no longer a product structure, but the breakdown of a functional requisite that was the basis for what should be bought.[8]

Standardization can either be the result of negotiations between stakeholders, e.g. within the International Standardization Organization, or become de facto standards, proprietary to a leading firm. In both cases standardization is subject to competition, because standards are actually ***defining the playing field of the market***.

Standards are not neutral, they are good or bad in achieving innovation, by introducing anarchic market relations into what was earlier controlled contract relations with sub-contractors or hierarchical structures within the company. The key question is:

---

[8] The problem of decoupling goes back to the Bourbaki-structures, developed by the French society of mathematicians, Bourbaki, in the 1920s and 30s (Corry, 1992). These structures, or group theory, became the basis for graph theory; implemented in engineering by e.g. Arnold Kaufmann, who was chief engineer at the French electrical utility EDF in the 1950s and 60s. In graph theory complexity is reduced by decoupling a large graph of dependencies into "islands", smaller graphs with minimum dependencies between them. Kaufmann (1967:312-315) showed the importance of delimiting complexity, by dis-associating networks into network islands, between which couplings are loose. Thompson (1967) brought this thought to organization theory, by his domain concept: the arena where a company can temporally focus without considering outside environmental dynamics. He was explicitly referring to Von Neumann, & Morgenstern (1944/2007) and Luce, & Raiffa (1957). In Wintelism, a loosely coupled product architecture permits components to be outsourced, based on an explicit limited set (a "brief") of knowledge. Von Hippel (1990) mistakenly ascribed such decoupling to Alexander (1964) and Simon (1976).

What decoupling promotes innovation to the benefit of the ultimate brand owner?

The decoupling of functional parts of products or services presumes that the dependencies between the elements linked by the standard are limited and known. If decoupling is done with a poor understanding of the dependences, the thus construed marketplace will fail, or the parties will have to adapt the supposedly standardized product or service to integrate it in its own offerings (Kjellström, 2019).

The product structure's effect on competition

The conception of the product structure is a condition of subsumption.

Functional structures do not homogenize competition; they stratify it. Functional decomposition allows different competitive logics to coexist within the same value chain. Some functions become standardized, substitutable and delivered under price competition.

Other functions remain integrative, knowledge-intensive, and under value-competition. Thus, subsumption is uneven. Capital subsumes functions, not the "firm as whole". Different labor processes can be fully commodified, partially subsumed, and temporarily protected.

Capital's ability to subsume labor increasingly depends on its ability to abstract production into structures that can be recomposed, rather than on direct control of labor alone.

Long waves in capitalism are not driven by "technology" as such, but by new ways of structuring production, which reconfigure subsumption, competition, and rent extraction.

2.6 Capital functions[9]

Capital functions are three fundamentally different tasks of capital: producing, market relating, and owning. The central question for transition theory is whether, and under what conditions, these functions can be partially appropriated by workers, without destroying the capitalist productive process.

Producing

Producing is the control and management of the production process, 'as is', with given environmental conditions. Those who perform these capital functions are the workers who perform the

---

[9] See Philipson (1980). I have revised the name of two of the concepts, without changing the content.

producing functions for capital: foremen, planners, time study men, other technicians, and engineers up to the production manager; together with the workers on the shop floor called the collective worker.

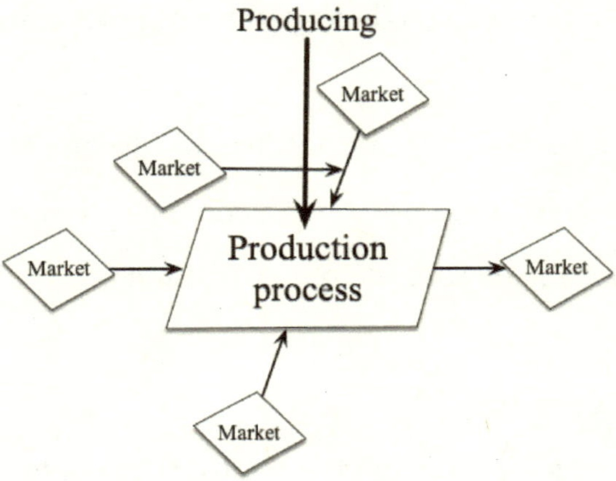

Figure 8. Producing.

Market relating

Market relating refers to the capital functions that relate to markets. Purchase of raw materials, semi-finished products, machinery or labor, or sale of finished products and services. All within environmental conditions given by the owning function, see below.

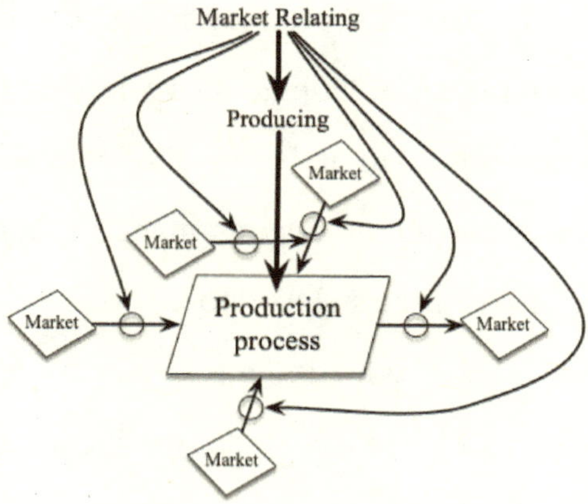

Figure 9. Market Relating.

Owning

The owning function determines what the capital is to be used for. In which markets should it be present, how it should conduct the business in general, and the choice of company management.

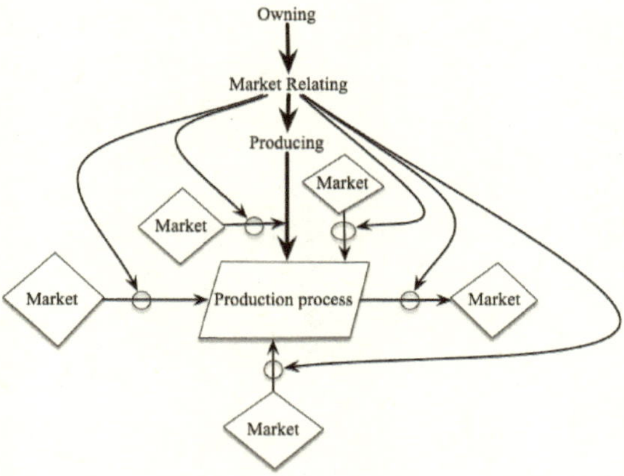

Figure 10. Owning.

Figure 11. Shows the capitalist production process as a whole, with the producing, market relating, and ownership functions; where each level is subsumed under the above level. The illustration tries to show the producing, market relating, and ownership functions as three superimposed "hats" on the capitalist production process. The production management controls the production process within "given" frameworks, i.e. already purchased raw materials, components and labor and that someone else (the market relating function) takes care of the procurement of the raw materials, the components, the labor force, and the sale of the finished products on a market). The market relating function determines these "boundary conditions" vis-à-vis the market, by making the purchases and being responsible for the sales. The ownership function decides on which markets the company should be, how the company should be managed and how decisions should be made.

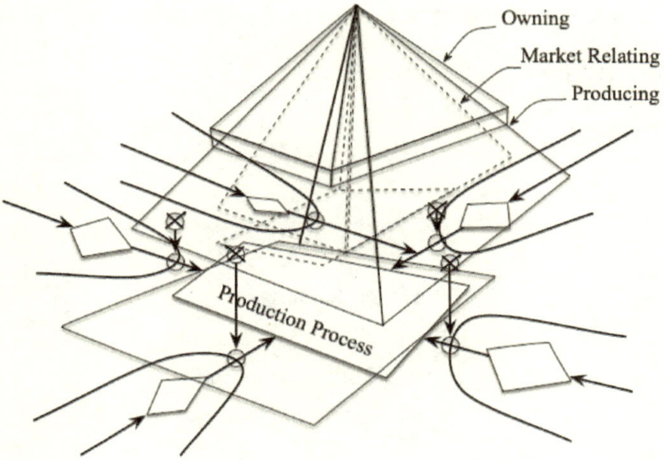

Figure 11. Capitalist production as a profit-making process.

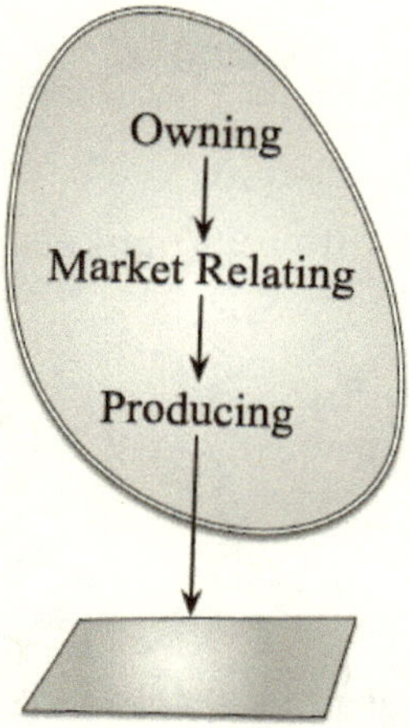

Figure 12. Simplified representation of Figure 11.

When the capital has experience of several producing functions, i.e. several factories, it can be illustrated in figure 13. It can e.g.

involve a factory in Sweden and one in China, but sales and purchases still take place collectively.

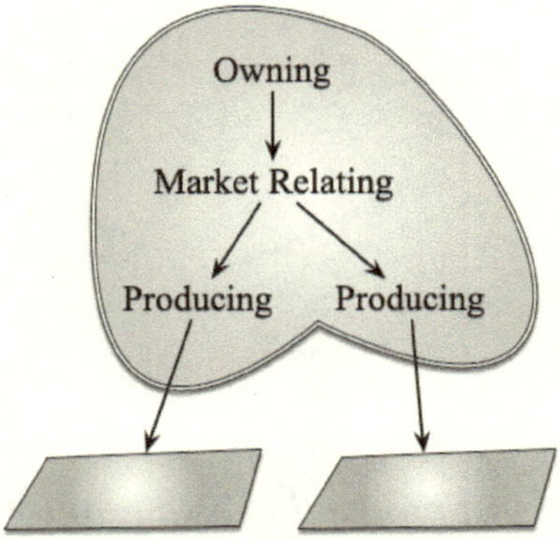

Figure 13. Capital with experience of several producing functions.

When sales take place in different markets, it can be illustrated as in Figure 9.

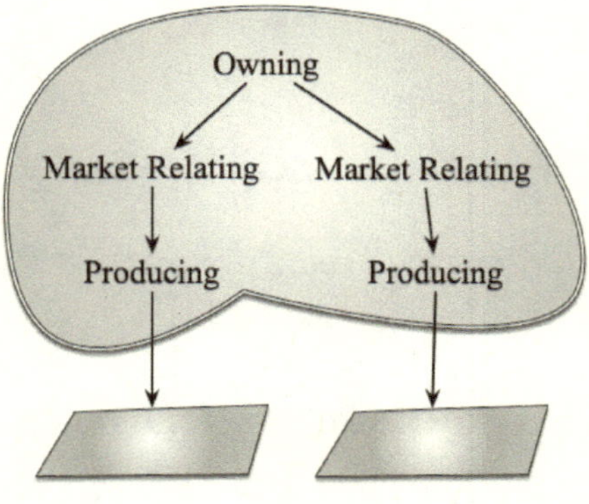

Figure 14. Capital with experience of relating to several markets.

When the experiences become more general, i.e. that the capital has experience of driving production and sales in many units and markets, it can be illustrated as in figure 15.

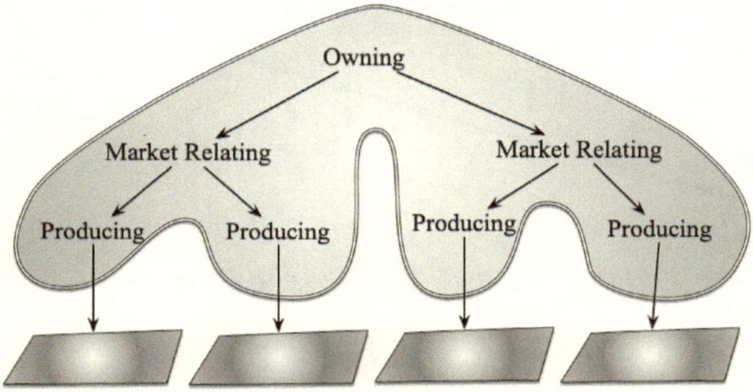

Figure 15. Generalized experience of producing and market relating functions.

Generalized capital functions

A measure of how advanced a capital is their experience of capital functions, how many different types of markets one has production in, how many purchasing and disposal markets one has experience of. And what types of businesses have capital been invested in.

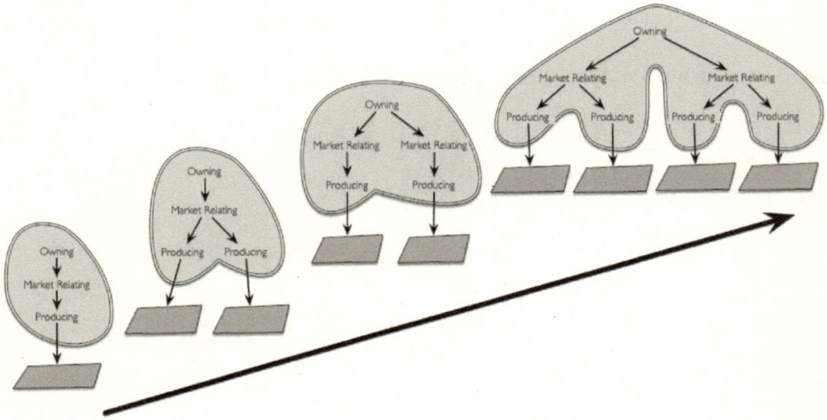

Figure 16. Generalized capital functions.

Financial capital

When the ownership itself is sublimated, subordinated to other ownership, when the company management of the owning company performs the capital function of ownership in a subordinate company, we speak of financial capital. Here, too, we can speak of more or less generalized experiences of financial capital functions. The simplest variant is illustrated in figure 17.

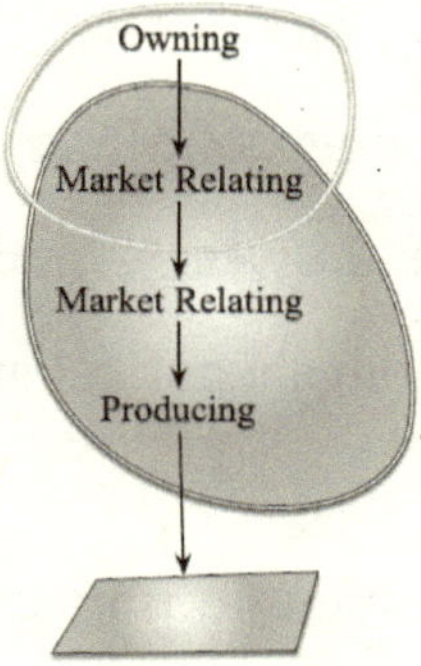

Figure 17. Simple financial capital.

The completed generalized financial capital is illustrated in figure 18. The profit of the individual company is accumulated in the financial capital, which leads to the ***concentration of capital***, see below in 2.7.

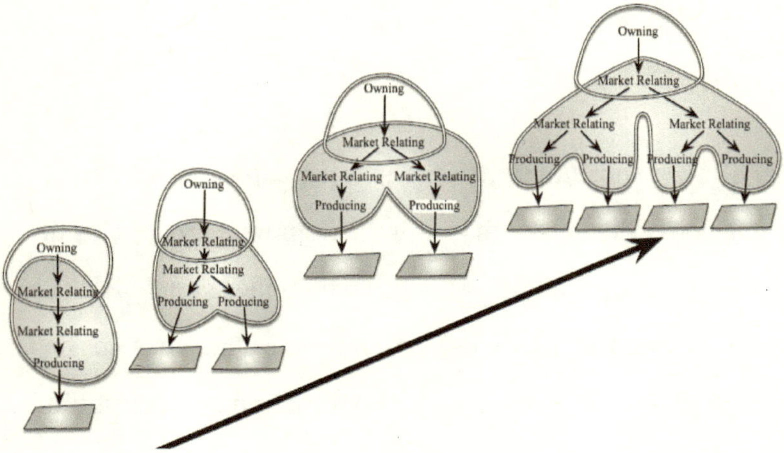

Figure 18. Generalized financial capital functions.

Summary of capital functions

Mechanical materialist readings of Marx, most prominently in Braverman and in Baran and Sweezy, interpret the subsumption of labor under capital as both ahistorical and all-encompassing. In these accounts, subsumption appears as a completed condition of mature capitalism, advancing uniformly and irreversibly toward total domination of labor by capital.

Marx's own analysis does not support this interpretation. Subsumption is a historical process, not a final state. It unfolds through specific forms of competition, organization, and control, and it operates unevenly across time, sectors, and functions. Crucially, subsumption does not occur "in general," but through concrete capital functions: producing, market-relating, and owning.

By analyzing subsumption at the level of capital functions, it becomes possible to identify both the dominant tendencies of capitalism and the conditions under which these tendencies are partially suspended, mediated, or contested. This does not negate capitalism's systemic drive toward abstraction and control; it explains how class struggle can temporarily redirect it. The capital functions framework is therefore not a denial of subsumption, but a historically grounded reconstruction of Marx's dialectical method.

2.7 Alienation

Capital's subsumption of the means of production, the work process and the products of the work process, creates alienation in the workers. The workers' influence on the immediate working conditions have generally diminished over time, in both capitalism or proto-socialist societies; their alienation, as an objective, not subjective concept (Øversveen, 2022) has increased, both under capitalism and in societies that proclaim to represent them. Socialist and Communist leaders have sought power over the state, in most cases with disastrous results for their alleged constituency, the working class.

For the theory of alienation to be compatible with the Marxist critique of capitalism, it needs to be able to (Øversveen, 2022: 5):

1. explain alienation as a specific feature of capitalist societies, rather than a universal suffrage and issue condition of human existence,
2. detail how alienation arises as an objective process from the organization of production, and
3. be compatible with a progressive political vision of a more socialized and less alienated form of society.

This is the objective result of capital's subsumption (Øversveen, 2022), which produces a subjective state of mind in the workers, where they cannot feel proud of their work and its result.

Øversveen (2022) correctly identifies the difference between the concept of the "young Marx" and the use of it after Marx has identified the fundamental laws of capitalism.

> *"...we produce an external reality that reflects our activity back to us in the form of worked matter that prescribes certain social imperatives, obligations and resistances."* (Øversveen, 2022: 7).

Thus, our social relations and our mind become a reflection of this objective reality.

2.8 The tendency of the profit quote to diminish

Marx showed that the profit quote tends to diminish within capitalism. Now and then, new fundamental technologies are invented (water mills, electricity, information technology, etc.), corresponding to the long waves of the Kondratieff cycles (Philipson, 2022b), allowing the profit quotes to increase for a period.

> *"... it is clear that the information technology revolutions managed to reverse the decline in the world output-capital*

ratio for a decade or two in the early 1990s, that effect quickly wore off." (Basu, Huato, Jauregui, & Wasner, 2022; Mediapart, 2023-01-07).

This does not change the fundamental tendency shown by Marx. It does neither hinder that fewer and fewer capitalists usurps more and more of these profits and becoming absurdly rich. So that fewer capitalists get more of the total mass of the profit is not contradictory to the tendency of diminishing profits.
The study of Basu *et al.* (2022) clearly shows how the average profit rate has fallen from almost 10% to around 6,5% in the 60 years between 1960 and 2019.

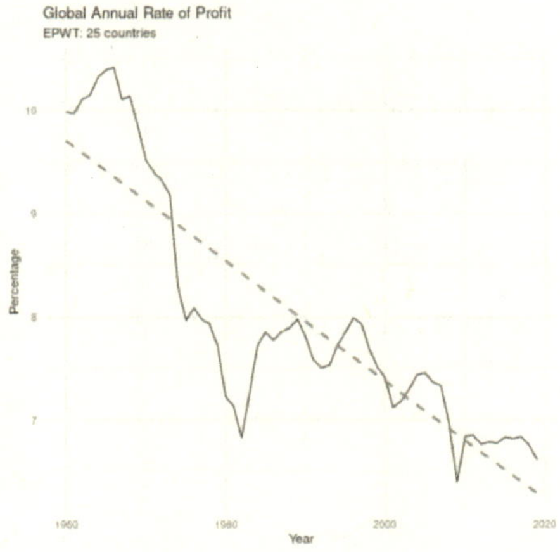

Figure 19. The falling rate of profit 1960-2019 (Basu et al., 2022)

2.9 Concentration of capital

Less drastic, but potentially as damaging, negative effects of capitalism are the ***concentration*** of industry, in a country or globally. Glattfelder (2010) showed that 50 corporations own 40% of global business. The consequences of concentration are less product and service differentiation (commoditization), hence less choice for customers, and that firms acquire monopoly rent above normal average profits. The combination of the generalization of capital is historically overrun by the concentration of capital. The problem with this is that it becomes more difficult to uncover the real political interests of highly concentrated capital. You need to be a fly, sitting on the roof in their board room…

We all know the ***environmental*** effects of production and consumption under capitalism (York, Rosa, & Dietz, 2003). Infringement of free speech, limiting access to public information, and limitations of democracy could also be counted as such effects.

Such tendencies could be countered by the active use of ***anti-trust law***, by individual and corporate social responsibility (by firms often referred to as sustainability) and by the actions of NGOs, political parties, and eventually states, and international treaties.

We discuss here the economic basis of this contradiction and what must be done to weaken the brutalizing forces and strengthen the democratizing forces. It shows why anarchist pipe dreams of going from capitalism to a democratic anarchy is just pipe dreams. It shows why a Stalinist socialism in a backward country will strengthen the brutalizing forces and weaken the democratizing forces. And it shows that soundly based in economic science.

Marx wrote the four major texts on political issues. These were: (1) Class struggles in France 1848 to 1850 (Marx, 1962), (2) The 18th Brumaire of Napoleon Bonaparte (Marx, 1979), (3) Civil war in France (Marx, 1972b), and (4) Critique of the Gotha program (Marx, 1970c). Of these only the latter two were written after he had made his major work on economic theory.

Although he posed that the political level was determined by the economic level, he never really worked out these relations. In none of his works did he analyze the differences within classes. To understand the democratic and brutalizing forces of capitalism it is necessary to understand the differences between different strata of the classes in capitalism.; that these different strata have economic interests which differ in such a way that they are more or less suitable for alliances to gain a democratic future. In my

1980 theses I started such a work, but have only now been able to continue.

2.10 Theoretical implications

Capitalism is defined by generalized competition among capitals. Competition operates primarily through price, driven by cost differentials, productivity comparisons, the organic composition of capital. Competition enforces profit-rate equalization pressures, centralization and concentration, and abstraction and standardization of labor. These tendencies describe capitalism's dominant long-run dynamics, not a temporally continuous process. The following chapter examines how these systemic tendencies have taken distinct historical form in successive sub-modes of capitalist production.

Chapter 2
Capitalism as a System
– Marx Theory of Capitalism
— Systemic Summary

Capitalism is a system driven by generalized competition among capitals.

Competition operates through different mechanisms, most prominently price-based competition, which enforces cost comparison, productivity pressure, and abstraction of labor.

These competitive mechanisms generate systemic tendencies toward concentration, centralization, and the subsumption of the work process under capital.

At the same time, capitalism also generates historically limited countertendencies, in which competition depends on differentiation, learning, and value creation rather than price alone.

3. Modes of Production under Capitalism

As capital's real subsumption evolves under capitalism, the mode of production evolves: There have been five major phases of the capitalist ***real subsumption*** (cf., Bettelheim; Philipson, 1980) of production: the publishing system, the direct control system, Taylorism, Fordism, and wintelism/globalism (sometimes called post-Fordism). There are indications that we are now entering into a fourth phase, with hitherto unknown character (Philipson, 2022b).

3.1 The publishing system

The publishing system, preceding the factory system, meant that the merchant bought fabrics and tools and let the individual laborer work in his home. During the absolute monarchy, the king gave a fief of a a local monopoly to manufacture supplies, mainly for the armed forces (rifles, cannons, uniforms, etc.). These mills were partially industrialized factories, but within a feudal power structure, rather than a market.

The capitalist had at that stage only subsumed the market relating function, i.e. the relations to markets. In this mode, workers still control the production function. Potentially the workers could still market relate by bringing the finished product to the market. But this is generally not possible, as they were impoverished peasants that had neither the capital to buy raw material nor tools. Even to get the products to the market would have been associate with costs.

3.2 The direct control system

During the transition between feudalism and capitalism, the workers were an immediate collective worker, selling the work force collectively to the capitalist with an elected contre-maître (opposing the master). This counter-master had the role of production manager and was hence not alienated from the workers.

The factory system meant that the workers were brought into the factory, a building owned by the capitalist. It permitted the capitalist or his representatives (production manager – and foremen in larger factories) to directly supervise the work workers. This is what Marx describes in the Capital. In this mode, workers' capacity to appropriate capital functions is. The workers were controlled by the capitalist or a manager he put in his place, but the control was only based on the implicit threat of being sacked. The producing function was largely still managed by the workers, while the market relating functions was subsumed by the capitalist. The potential to take control of the market relating functions, as in the publishing system, no longer existed.

3.3 Taylorism

Taylorism, or scientific management as Taylor called it, was envisaged as a scientific “neutral” approach standing above the classes. Taylorism was the application of the machine-oriented discipline of engineering to labor relations (Maier, 1970: 30); it was ***the real subsumption of the work of the individual worker***. Not surprisingly, the supposedly impartial findings of science tended to confirm the approach of management, not labor. (Maier, 1970:31).

Then capitalism enforced the sale of the working power to be individual. The relations between workers were decided by the capitalist, or the person he put in his place, the production manager. But the skills of the workers were still artisanal or semi-artisanal. As the capitalists began to buy the labor individually, the capitalist also engaged a production manager.

In the US first and then in Europe, Taylorism was introduced with mean-time measurement, variable wages, and workers' loss of control of the immediate work process. Taylorism deskilled the worker and made him dependent on the machine or even when it was still manual, to the capitalist’s definitions of each small task. It ignored the experience of the worker and treated him as limbs of the capitalist head. In this mode, workers’ capacity to appropriate capital functions is low. The producing function is completely subsumed by capital, by forcing the worker to carry out narrowly defined tasks at a high pace, also with the implicit threat of losing the job. The work organization is often completely individualized. Taylorism is an efficiency-improving producing model for price-based competition.

3.4 Fordism

Fordism re-collectivized the workers around the mowing belt or the chemical process. But the collectivity, the collaboration, was one imposed by the capitalist.

While Taylorism concerned only the management of labor, Ford's doctrines stressed reorganization of ***the entire productive process*** (Maier, 1970: 54). The core production model of Fordism was mass production of ***standardized products,*** using forecast-driven, batch production (Vidal, 2019: 180-181). In this mode, workers' capacity to appropriate capital functions is also low. The subsumption of the workers in a by the capitalist defined work process increased the efficiency compared to Taylorism and was also a model for producing under price-based competition.

3.5 Wintelism

The post-Fordist[10] period can be dated roughly from the early 1980s to the present, following a decade of industrial restructuring, including offshoring of manufacturing, financialization, vertical disintegration and de-unionization (Vidal, 2019: 181).

The transition of the leading economic powers to the post-industrial era in the late twentieth century shifted focus in the production systems to new dimensions of productivity and organizational efficiency, such as innovation, creativity, networking, group organization, and value-based leadership. Those dimensions were not a part of Taylorism and contradicted much of it. Many of its principles and techniques (maximum division of labor, detailed monitoring of individual time and motions, focus on an individual, not a group, etc.) turned out to be

---

[10] Sandberg called this Toyotism and held that its superior productivity must be understood as a product of design-for-assembly, and long-term relations with sub-contractors and with the core of highly educated workers. The subcontractor system with networks for production and development work is efficient and the low costs are further reduced, due to lower wages and inferior job security and working conditions on lower levels in the subcontractor pyramid. Such a dual labor market is particularly alien to the traditional Swedish labor market model of solidaristic wages, with national agreements independent of company. (Sandberg, 1994: 157) I disagree with much of this description of the mode and hold that its characteristics are not fundamentally based on lower salaries. I have written in detail about these characteristics (Philipson, 2022a)

much less applicable to innovative industries of the post-industrial era (Grachev, & Rakitsky, 2013: 516).

To traditional "leftist" researchers, the development of capitalism is the mechanical results of the economy:

> *Tony Smith demonstrated that even under lean production, structural coercion and the real subsumption of labor remain. Although workers under lean production may experience real increases in decision-making authority, including process control, standard setting, safety, scheduling and training, the set of issues is limited to pre-given parameters (Vidal, 2019:189).*

> *The key issues regarding skill and empowerment concern the focus of local management and the orientation and power of the local workforce. Even where managers intend to empower their workers, the pressure to maintain tight process control and get products out the door makes it difficult for them to find time to train workers and devolve responsibility (Vidal, 2019: 189).*
> *The emphasis is not on outcomes (efficiency versus valorization), but on functions (coordination versus discipline). A managerial focus on discipline can lead to an emphasis on securing physical surplus labor – a*

> *limited type of valorization – rather than overall valorization of physical and intellectual labor (Vidal, 2019: 190).*

> *The workers empowerment will be limited to concerns with process or product improvement, while traditional management will continue to be the ultimate authority, ready to exercise a veto or remove (partial) worker empowerment at any time (Vidal, 2019: 192).*

This mechanistic description of the evolution of capitalism does not give any room for class struggle to bring capitalism in any other direction, or that the working class manages to do so, the influence gained is supposed to be of no importance.

The character of this mode of production is the transformation from physical control to a focus on value creation. If Taylorism and Fordism both focused on the subsumption of the work process, Wintelism meant that capital came to focus on value creation itself. In value creation, workers' tacit knowing and explicit knowledge might help capital to increase the value that he can deliver to the customer; hence the workers can potentially trade their knowing and their knowledge against a certain amount of influence. In this mode, workers' capacity to appropriate capital functions are contradictory, sometimes (in some parts of the firm and the value-chain) moderate to high, in other parts, operating under price-based logic, low. Which competitive logic dominates therefore depends not only on the firm, but on which capital function is exposed to which market.

Chapter 3
Modes of Production under Capitalism — Systemic Summary

The capitalist mode of production progressively subsumes the forces of production, reorganizing them in accordance with the requirements of valorization.

This subsumption is historically uneven: it differs across capitals and operates asymmetrically across the producing, market-relating, and owning functions within a single capital.

4 Price- vs Value-based Competition

This chapter reconstructs the objective coexistence of price- and value-based competition within capitalism; its implications for class struggle is developed later. Which competitive logic dominates therefore, depends not only on the firm, but on which capital function is exposed to which market.

Value-based competition appears here not as an anomaly, but as capitalism's historically recurring counter tendency.

Capitalist competition is either price-based or value-based. Price-Based competition is the systemic properties of capitalism, as shown by Marx. He introduced a quantitative measure of how advanced a capital is, the organic opposition of capital, i.e. the relation between constant capital and total capital.

When a capital had a higher organic composition than its competitors, it lifted a rent, by redistribution of profits in the market, so that the individual firm got the proportion of the total profits in the market in proportion to its organic composition.

The resulting concentration, that firms with higher organic composition got more and more of the market (oligopoly and eventually monopoly), eventually resulted in a lower profit quote and on the systemic level a crisis of capitalism.

Value-based competition is competition in a highly competitive market, mostly when no company has a dominant position. The firms compete by delivering better value to the customers. Ricardo had seen value-based competition as equally systemic as price-based competition. Marx was not foreign to value-based competition but held that it is not systemic, but temporal.

4.1 Price-based competition as the dominant systemic logic

Price-based competition is not a choice, but a structural imperative. It disciplines firms, managers, and workers alike. It suppresses slack, learning, and diversity of production forms, it tends toward deskilling scale advantages and market concentration.

However, this describes capitalism as a system, not capitalism at every moment.

4.2 The dual logic of competition; real subsumption is function specific

Modern competition is function-specific, rather than firm-wide. Because producing, market-relating, and owning functions are structurally distinct, price-based and value-based competition coexist both within individual firms and across value chains. These functions are separable and unevenly subsumed. This coexistence is made possible by product and function architectures that separate competitive logics across different parts of production. It is precisely this structural separation that explains why Ricardian value-based rent persists even under intensified competition.

Function-specific competition follows from the structural separation of producing, market-relating, and owning functions.

The competitive form is jointly determined by structural position in production (capital functions, product architecture), and historical–cyclical market conditions (tight vs slack labor markets, boom vs depression).

Cheap access to skilled labor is not the same as sustained capability formation. In depression knowledge is available, but learning is not protected, retention is not guaranteed, collective experience is fragile, and tacit coordination does not accumulate.

Thus, capital can buy capabilities, but it cannot reproduce it cheaply. Depressions temporarily convert value relations into price relations expansions reassert capability scarcity.

Competition oscillates between price-dominant and value-dominant forms depending on market tightness – but the production of value remains structurally grounded in capabilities. The implications of this temporal oscillation for class struggle and transition is developed later.Capitalism has evolved and the outsourcing of the production of components has evolved to what is sometimes called Ecosystems.

To optimize the value of the offering, the focal firm (with direct relation to the end market) view the value chain as an ecosystem, which they try to align with their conception of the final offering. The other parties of the ecosystem cooperate in producing value and are at same time competing about catching a large share of the value of the offering and their respective roles in producing the offering.

The ecosystem is the alignment structure of the multilateral set of partners that need to interact for a focal value proposition to materialize (Adner, 2017: 40). This definition places the value proposition as the foundation of the ecosystem (Adner, 2017: 43).

This extends the consideration of the ecosystem, beyond the question of value creation and value capture, to the question of value distribution across the broader ecosystem and the extent to which it is treated as a matter of bargaining or as a strategic lever in the ecosystem construction (Adner, 2017: 56). This redistribution of value corresponds to the mechanisms of monopoly rent (Smith, 1776/1982; Malthus, 1798/1970; Ricardo, 1817/1971; Marx, 1894/1970; Schumpeter, 1947; Von Hippel, 1988).

Ecosystems give capitalism a large degree of (conditional) planning. Different such ecosystems compete of the end-user, but the strength of these ecosystems help to concentrate capital.

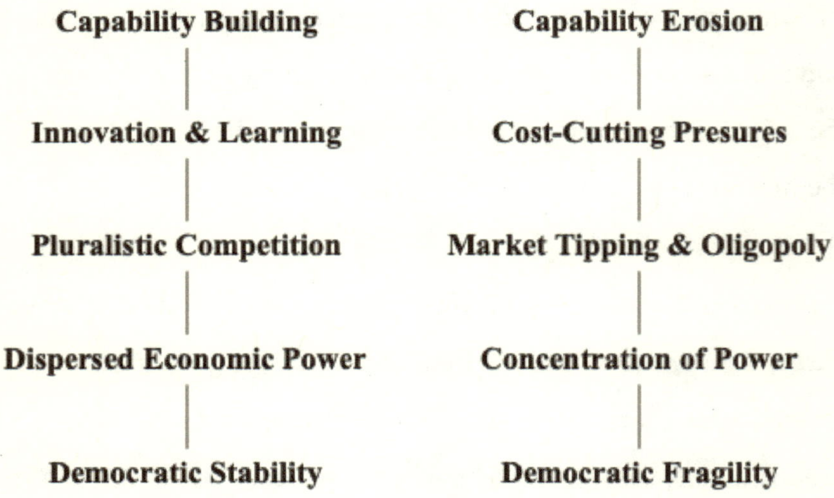

Figure 20. Dual Logics of Capitalism: Value-Based and Price-Based Competition.

4.3 Even though value-based competition is only temporal, it always exists

Capitalism does not move toward a single logic of competition. It produces structured coexistence of price and value-based competition, mediated by product and function architectures. by product and function.

Functional decomposition enables capital to subject some activities to price-based competition, while shielding others within value-based competition, thereby stabilizing rent extraction even as overall competition intensifies.
This is why ecosystems exist and why focal firms capture rent It is also the reason why suppliers are disciplined by price and why workers' knowledge matters only in some functions.

Whether competition takes a value-based or price-based form is also conditioned by the state of the market. In periods of depression, capital can acquire highly educated and experienced labor-power at very low exchange values. Under such conditions, firms may appear to compete on price while still accessing advanced capabilities. However, this does not abolish value-based competition. Capability formation, retention, and cumulative learning cannot be sustained through market purchase alone. Once markets tighten, the scarcity of experienced labor reasserts itself, and competitive advantage again depends on the internal development of productive forces. Depressions thus temporarily mask value-based competition; they do not eliminate it.

Market conditions modulate how competition appears, but not what ultimately produces value. Depressions temporarily convert value into price, but cannot reproduce the capabilities on which value-based competition rests.

Price-based and value-based competition structurally coexist, this is not transition theory.

We will later show that class struggle is not only a struggle over wages and work conditions, but also a struggle over which functions are value-based.

Dimension	Value-Based Capitalism (VBC)	Price-Based Capitalism (PBC)
Theory of value	Productive, objective surplus	Marginal utility, subjective
Firm behavior	Innovation, learning, differentiation	Cost minimization, scale
Competition	Dynamic, evolutionary	Static, price-based equilibrium
Market structure	Open-ended rivalry	Tendency toward oligopoly
Role of capabilities	Central	Irrelevant
Profit source	Innovation & surplus generation	Temporary deviations from equilibrium

Table 2. Contrasting the two types of competition

4.4 Example of value-based rent, the redistribution of value over the market[11]

Classical economics (Smith, 1776/982; Malthus, 1798/1970; Ricardo, 1817/1971; Marx 1894/1970; and others) understood that there is a drive among capitalists to get more than the average profit. They recognized this as monopoly rent, a premium for being different, which meant that profits were re-distributed in the marketplace to the advantage of the company with a unique, and especially the most unique product. To begin this was supposed to be because of monopoly control of natural resources. Ricardo is credited with the clearest analysis of land rent. Marx (1894/1970; 1970, 1973) used Ricardo's concept for land rent for industrial capitalism. He introduced the concept of redistribution of profits by the organic composition of capital, a measure for how advanced the capital is in in employing science and technology. Schumpeter (1942, 1947) used the term monopoly rent in a sense akin to Marx' concept, to explain the "long waves" of capitalism and fundamental effects of entrepreneurial "destructive changes"; when market conditions are fundamentally changed by the innovations of "entrepreneurs" (cf. Elliott, 1980). The entrepreneur gains a temporary monopoly rent by being unique (von Hippel, 1988).

---

[11] See Philipson (2020b) and Philipson (2022)

This can be illustrated by the monopoly rent that Apple was able to gain by the introduction of the iPhone in mid 2007, illustrated in figure 21. In 2006, Nokia caught 60% of the profits in the market for mobile telephone terminals. Four years later, Apple had 75% of the profits and Nokia zero. Two years later Nokia, the monopolist six year earlier, had been forced out of the market.

Despite what is commonly thought, given the increasing Android sales, Apple has increased its dominance, see table 3. In 2016, Apple took 92% of the profits in the market, although Samsung is the leader in terms of market share, but does not earn any money! Google is the profit leader for operating systems (Android), but that does not trickle down to its partners using that operating system. Hence, even if a company has a smaller market share, it can catch the lion's share of the profit, because of the monopoly rent gained by differentiation. This also illustrates the important difference between market share, share of total sales in industry, and profit share, share of the total profits in industry. The market share does not tell who the industry leader is.

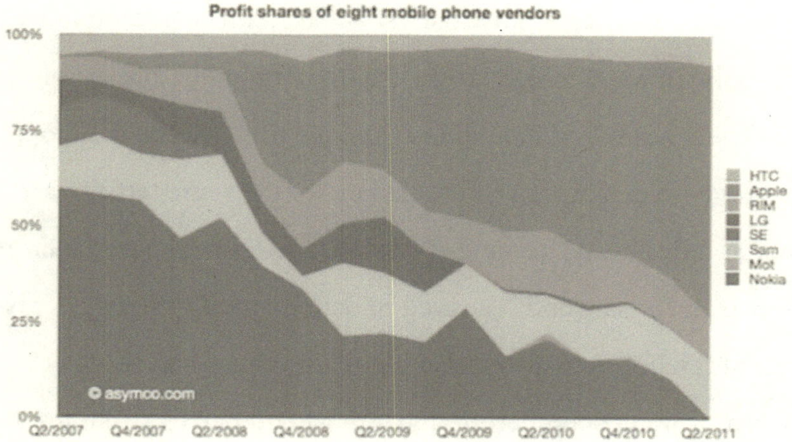

Figure 21. Profits in the Mobile Phone Vendor Market, Asymco (2013-06-28)

Global Smartphone Profit by Vendor	Operating Profit Share (%)
Apple	91.0%
Huawei	2.4%
Vivo	2.2%
OPPO	2.2%
Others	2.2%
Total	100.0%

Table 3. Global Smartphone Operating Profit Share in Q3 2016, Strategic Analytics (2016-11-25).

Monopoly interest is the excess profit that a particularly competitive individual capital realizes (gets) against the average profit in the specific market, based on organic composition, innovations, etc. Monopoly interest is the result of a (temporary) monopoly. In Marx's time it was usually monopoly interest on land. The piece of land ten miles from the town where the crops were sold yielded more profit than land of the same fertility a hundred miles away, because it was cheaper to transport the crop to the town for sale and it arrived in better condition. Today, it is a result of the differentiation (making the products and services different from the competitors) that most companies strive for, to avoid the products becoming standard product (goods). Standard goods, or homogeneous products that differ only in price, but not in value, are the result of the neo-classical economists' 'perfect competition', a theoretical model that seldom exists in reality. An example of such a product is buying an unspecified ton of wheat on the Chicago Stock Exchange.

Rent can also be captured from the supply chain. To my knowledge there are no systematic studies of value catching in the supply chain. The reason is that it requires access to the internal accounting of many companies. An example shows that Apple has a gross margin of 40%, while their main smartphone producer Foxconn only has only single digit gross margins (Macrumors, 2024-05-01). This probably indicates that Apple catches value from the value chain. In most cases the ***focal firm*** (the one at the end of the value chain, delivering value to the end customer) is often and probably mostly the company that can take advantage of of the value chain for reaping rent.

Chapter 4
Price- vs Value-based Competition — Systemic Summary

Capitalist competition operates through two distinct logics.

In price-based competition, profits are redistributed through productivity differentials and the organic composition of capital.

In value-based competition, profits are redistributed through differentiated use-values, yielding Ricardian rents grounded in learning, capability, and coordination.

5. Classes and Strata

Kautsky reduced Marxist analysis to the fight between the two main classes of the capitalist system, proletariat and capital. Kautsky's analysis of political power is organized around the key issues of class polarization and working-class unity in capitalist society. (Shandro, 1997/1998:481). There was no need to make concrete analysis of different strata in the two classes, as they always were supposed to act as homogeneous unities. This is fundamentally wrong, both for the working class[12] and the capitalist class[13]. The class is supposed to be class in itself, without separate interests for different strata.

The analysis that I propose is necessary to understand the complexities of "the collective worker", the differentiation within the working class. In the citation from Marx below, he makes clear that ***all*** the elements of the collective worker are productive workers, not only the one running the machinery or transporting the raw material, but also the lab-workers and the engineer!

---

[12] *"...der eine mehr mit der Hand, der andre mehr mit dem Kopf arbeitet, der eine als manager, engineer, Technolog etc., der andre als overlooker, der dritte |66| als direkter Handarbeiter, oder gar bloss Handlanger, so werden mehr und mehr Funktionen von Arbeitsvermögen unter den unmittelbaren Begriff der produktiven Arbeit und ihre Träger unter den Begriff der produktiven Arbeiter..." (Marx, 1969a: 65-66)*

[13] *"...il peut y avoir des différences d'intérêts au sein de la classe des capitalists industriels; notament entre les chefs d'entreprises de l'industrie lorde [department I] et les chefs d'entreprise de l'industrie légère [department II]." (Bettelheim, 1971a: 8)*

Whether they have a class consciousness or not. This chapter therefore defines strata by relation to surplus-value production and capital-functions.

For Marx the classes were not unified unless they became unified in class struggle. The very objective of a working-class party is to seek the unification of the working class. But this cannot be done by denying differences, of both interests and positions, a unity of diverse interests.

"The notion of community, with its connotation of unity in diversity, provides a better metaphor for working-class unity than does the notion of consciousness." (Shandro, 1997/1998:499).

However, Shandro is mistaken in that it is not either community or consciousness. It also means that class is not more important than identity, it is unity of diverse identities[14].

5.1 The working class

Marx' view was not that the working class consisted of the industrial workers, but of the productive workers, who produce surplus value for a capitalist. It is not a question of how much

---

[14] If the class struggle means that different groups, whether black, hbtq, etc. are not allowed to aspire for bourgeois democratic rights within capitalism, but must wait for a distant socialist future, they will not enter under the unity. An example is the Jüdische Arbeiter Bund, which Lenin forbid the participation in his project, see below.

workers earn, but what role they have in capitalism as an economic system. The working class consists of ***productive*** workers. By that is meant the workers who perform their work ***under capitalist conditions of production***, i.e. work to create surplus value for the capitalist. It has nothing to do with whether the work is poorly paid, what training is needed or whether the result of the work has materialized in a product or a service.

Workers are those that are part of the ***collective worker***, which includes the whole hierarchy from the worker at the assembly line, over the engineer, to the production manager. The latter, however, will be affected by the fact that they also perform capital functions on behalf of the capitalist. They will therefore be politically divided:

> *"Included among these productive workers, of course, are those who contribute in one way or another to the production of the commodity, from the actual operative to the manager or engineer (as distinct from the capitalist)."* (Marx, 1970a: 156-157).
>
> *"Not only the labourer working directly with his hands on the machine, but the overlooker, engineer, manager, clerk, etc.- in a word, the labour of the whole personnel required in a particular sphere of material production to produce a particular commodity, whose joint labour (co-operation)*

> *is required for commodity production."* (Marx, 1969b: 164)

Marx made no distinction between the ***content of the work***. The goods can be manifested in ***physical products or services***.

> *"When we speak of the commodity as a materialization of labor – in the sense of its exchange-value – this itself is only an imaginary, that is to say, a purely social mode of existence of the commodity which has nothing to do with its corporeal reality; it is conceived as a definite quantity of social labor or of money. It may be that the concrete labor whose result it is leaves no trace in it."* (Marx, 1969b: 171)

> *"...when Marx defined productive labor, he completely abstracted from its content, from the concrete, useful character and result of the labor. He treated labor only from the standpoint of its social form. Labor which is organized in a capitalist enterprise is productive labor. The concept "productive," as well as the other concepts of Marx's political economy, have a historical and social character. For Marx productive labor means: labor which is engaged in the given social system of production."* (Rubin, 1973/1990: 272).

> The *"...singer commissioned by an entrepreneur to sing in order to make money for him is a productive laborer; for she produces capital."* (Rubin, 1973/1990: 273).

There is no difference between manual and intellectual work
Not only the laborer working directly with his hands or a machine, but the foreman, the engineer, the manager, the clerk, etc. – in a word, the labor of the whole personnel required in a particular sphere of material production. In fact, they add their aggregate labor to the constant capital and increase the value of the product by this amount (Marx, 1969b: 164).

The same kind of work can be productive or unproductive

> *"...the designation of labor as productive labor has absolutely nothing to do with the determinate content of that labor, its special utility, or the particular use-value in which it manifests itself. The same kind of labor may be productive or unproductive."* (Marx, 1969b: 401)
> *"...the cooks and waiters in a public hotel are productive laborers, in so far as their labor is transformed into capital for the proprietor of the hotel." (Marx, 1969b: 159).*

> *"If we may take an example from outside the sphere of production of material objects, a schoolmaster is a productive labourer, when, in addition to be labouring the heads of his scholars, he works like a horse to enrich the school proprietors. That the latter has laid out his capital in a teaching factory, instead of a sausage factory, does not alter the relation.'* (Marx, 1970a: 509).

The result of the work can be products and services that are ***necessary***, ***luxury*** or ***destructive*** (e.g., weapons).

> *"The nature of such wants, whether, for instance, they spring from the stomach or from fancy, makes no difference."* (Marx.1970a: 35).

Transport, packing, and storage labor is productive, but trade is not productive, because it is carried out ***for the merchant capital***, not for ***the productive capital***. But concrete firms can be a ***mix*** of production and trade, which means that workers in the same firm can be productive (warehouse workers) and unproductive (the cashier at the supermarket checkout), or the same worker might have parts of his working day that is productive and other parts that is unproductive.

Most often, wholesale trade contains greater elements of productive work than retail trade, as transportation and packaging, i.e. bringing to the market, than sales, relating to the market.

> *"...the transport industry, transporting either people or commodities. The relation of productive labour – that is, of the wage-labourer – to capital is here exactly the same as in other spheres of material production. Moreover, here a material change is effected in the object of labour – a spatial change, a change of place."* (Marx, 1969b: 412).

> *"Commercial capital, therefore – stripped of all heterogeneous functions, such as storing, expressing, transporting, distributing, retailing, which may be connected with it, and confined to its true function of buying in order to sell – creates neither value nor surplus value..."* (Marx 1970c: 282).

Unproductive labor is labor that does not result in surplus value for a capitalist. If he is rich enough and can afford a servant, a driver or a house, that work is unproductive. If he buys cleaning twice a week from a dry-cleaning company, the work in the dry-cleaning company is productive, because the entrepreneur who has hired the cleaner does it to acquire added value.

Unproductive labor is the

> *"...labour which is not exchanged with capital, but directly with revenue, that is, with wages or profit (including of course the various categories of those who share as co-partners in the capitalist's profit, such as interest and pure)."* (Marx 1969b: 157).

Unproductive work can be ***necessary*** and ***materialized***. It's just not productive for the capitalist.

There is also work that is neither productive nor unproductive, that is simply not done within the framework of the capitalist mode of production: in reproduction, in simple commodity production, and in some parts of society where still feudal production remains.

Artisans and farmers are not productive workers. But they are neither unproductive:

> *"They therefore belong neither to the category of productive or unproductive labourers, although they are producers of commodities. But their production does not fall under the capitalist mode of production."* (Marx, 1969b: 407).

"Productive labour, in its meaning for capitalist production, is wage-labour which, exchanged against variable capital (the part of the capital that is spent on wages), reproduces not only this part of the capital (or the value of its own labour power), but in addition products surplus-value for the capitalist." (Marx, 1969b: 152)

5.2 Strata in the working class

1. The traditional industrial working class
2. Service workers under 'factory' conditions
3. Workers who also perform capital functions, mainly various office workers, engineers, economists, personnel consultants, in productive enterprises. They are the last part of the working class to be radicalized. They tend to support the bourgeoisie.
4. Service workers who work individually (bus drivers, property managers, etc.) in their own companies and are engaged in simple commodity production (petty bourgeoisie).
5. The lumpenproletariat (unemployed, who survive on petty theft, begging, prostitution, etc.) tend to support fascists,

when they don't see a politics from the left that gives them an apparent future.[15]

Strata of the collective worker that don't identify as workers

For the strata 3) and 4) above, it is more difficulty to reach class consciousness, because they do not live in a collective environment. Joint struggle in one's own workplace is more difficult, although not impossible.

Workers with temporary employment and part-time workers

Temporary employment is more common among women, young people, people born abroad and among people with pre-secondary education (International Labour Organization, 2015).

Worker entrepreneurs

The forklift truck driver can now be a hired self-employed person (interview with Åke Lamm, 2020-01-15). The reasons can be several:

---

[15] In the wake of the closure of the coal mining industry in England, the coal miners become lumpenproletariat and voted for Brexit. In the wake of the closure of the coal and metal industries, workers in northern France and the Massif Central voted for the Front National's racism against Arabs, despite the fact that there are very few Arabs in their areas, while southern France, with the most Arabs outside Paris, does not vote for the Front National to the same extent, despite the fact that most of the 'Pieds-Noirs' (some 3.2 million French nationals, who were thrown out of the Maghreb during the liberation of North Africa, and who generally are reactionary) live there. In the wake of the closure of the steel and metal industry in Bergslagen, a Swedish lumpenproletariat votes for the fascist Sweden Democrats.

1. Personal petty-bourgeois aspirations.
2. Deliberate attempts by capital to divide the working class.
3. The need to manage a difficult situation with short-term housing and part-time work. As a self-employed person, it is easier to get a job at several workplaces.

Workers with temporary employment and part-time workers
Temporary employment is more common among women, young people, people born abroad and among people with pre-secondary education (International Labour Organization, 2015).

Workers that perform functions of capital

The workers in the upper part of the hierarchy of the collective worker often performs functions of capital, making them susceptible to a deformed class consciousness. But they are important to win for the struggle or at least to become allies, as they have knowledge that is important to absorb by the collective. Some, as the foremen, could be absorbed by putting in place a shop-steward system, rotating the job between experienced workers.

All three variants reduce the strength of the organization, and the union should not be passive about absorbing or aligning them.

5.3 The false narrative of the north – south conflict

A populist left hold that the "real" contradictions are between the global north and the global south. The underlying assumption is that value is produced by colonial appropriation, rather than capitalist production. The anti-colonial north-south perspective is inspired by Rosa Luxemburg's revisionism of Marx (Luxemburg, 1913/1963), where she argued that capitalism could not exist without the imperialist theft of third world natural resources. Sure, Europe and the USA have stolen enormous wealth, above all in Africa and South America, but her analysis is based on a misunderstanding of Marx's theory building, drawing completely wrong conclusions about how the economic system works (Luxemburg, 1913/1963; Ödman, 1985). Her revisionism also led her to believe that capitalism would collapse by itself. Considering this anti-colonial populism, it is the United States and the states of Europe that are the enemies.

Another misconception within the left is immutability of imperialism. The old colonial powers are and remain colonial powers. But the majority are no longer. Belgium, Spain and Germany have long had no colonial dominance anywhere in the world. And the politically anything but dexterous Macron has now lost all French influence in Africa. Only a few island kingdoms remain in the Pacific. England has also largely lost all influence. Remaining the great devil, USA.

Instead, it is above all Russia and China that have emerged as imperialist nations. The two dominate Africa today, where they extract minerals and cultivate land for food for their own populations. Often the local population is exploited in slave-like conditions, as in the Chinese Cobalt mines, or by terrorist armies (Wagner). In South America, China now competes with the United States for influence, in the Middle East Russia competes with the United States, and in Central Asia China and Russia (Philipson, 2022b).

5.4 False reclassification: "middle strata"

In Bernstein's critic of Kautsky, diversity was more important than unity, as he saw capitalism evolving away from the importance of the classes. This group, which played such a big role in how both the 70s and todays left perceive class society. Poulantzas (1978) believed that the middle strata consist of the higher strata of the collective worker and the unproductive workers.

Following Bernstein, Poulantzas (1970), Therborn (1971; 1972) and Sunesson (1974), invented a new "class", the middle strata, which does not exist in Marx theory. These middle strata were considered to be the main ally of the proletariat, or even to be completely replacing the proletariat, as the base for so called left parties, in the wake of a wrongfully[16] perceived disappearing proletariat. Therborn (1971: 162-163) held that one category consists of holders of roles, whose coordinating and leading tasks are simultaneously determined by the work process and the conditions of production and exploitation specific to a given mode of production, roles which are to varying degrees simultaneously subordinate to and executors of the specific way in which surplus work is produced[17]. (Example: supervisor and engineer in a factory).

Another category consists of holders of roles, whose position in the labor process is to varying degrees similar to that of the direct producers but who do not directly produce surplus labor. Examples are non-productive, in the sense that their unpaid surplus labor for the employer does not produce surplus value for the capitalist economy, wage workers such as commercial employees, non-promoted clerical staff and menial staff for other types of private and public services.

---

[16] See the class analysis of Sweden below.

[17] Therborn develops this argument in his early Swedish work, prior to his later English-language class analyses.

As we have gone through above, according to Marx, the first group is a stratum within the working class. The second group is distinguished not because they perform services, but whether they are productive, unproductive or simply outside of capitalist production. They mainly comprise three groups:

1. Officials in the state and municipality who administer the state apparatus. They are politically undecided.
2. Police and military, the state's repressive apparatus. They are indeterminate, but tend to ally with the bourgeoisie, or in times of war or intensifying class struggle tend (because of their potentially repressive role) to ally with fascism.

Service workers in reproduction (nursing staff, teachers, etc. They tend to ally with the working class, but are stratified depending on social position, biography, etc. The nursing assistant has a clearer tendency to ally with the working class than the doctor and the high school teacher.[18]

Under special circumstances, layers may behave differently than expected.

---

[18] In 1974, a movement within the Portuguese military, the Movimento das Forças Armadas, MFA, overthrew the Portuguese dictator Salazar and introduced democracy (Wikipedia, 2026-01-11)

5.5 Strata in the capitalist class

The strata of the capitalist class reflect their position in the capitalist system:

1. Whether they compete in a price- or value-based market.
2. Their position in the total production system, whether they belong to department I or II, and to which sub-department they belong.
3. If they are productive or circulating capital.
4. The organic composition of their capital, i.e. roughly how advanced they are.
5. Their degree of centralization, roughly how much capital they control.
6. Their level of experience with generalized capital functions.

5.6 The petty bourgeoisie

The petty bourgeoisie consists of artisans, small shop owners, small industries, small service companies and small farmers. The emphasis on small is an expression of the fact that they are 'survival businesses' for the family, simple commodity production. They are marked, as the capitalist class, in their political tendencies by what their target market is, department I, department II or service directly to reproduction. A restaurant that has working-class customers tends to ally itself with the working class, as did many restaurants and hotel owners in Germany during the early 20th century. Another main mediator of their political interests is their economic situation. In booms, they often ally themselves with the capitalist class, which they then most resemble. In the recession with the working class. But if they face an acute threat of proletarianization, they may ally themselves with a fascism that paints the liquidation of real or imagined enemies.

It is important not to alienate the petty bourgeoisie. Their dual determination, as both workers and capitalists, allows them to ally with the working class as well as the democratic or fascist bourgeoisie. Depending on our policies, they can either give us or our worst enemy strength.

Chapter 5
Classes and Strata
— Systemic Summary

Classes are determined by their position in the relations of production.

Within each class there are distinct strata, with different material conditions and interests.

Only through political unification do these strata constitute a class capable of collective action.

6. Contemporary Class Structure, Sweden

This chapter therefore reconstructs Swedish class structure using Marxian categories rather than occupational ones.

6.1 The limits of existing class analyses

After Therborn's (1972) analysis, no proper review has been made of the classes in Sweden. Therborn's analysis is highly problematic. As we have shown above, it is not ***what*** people ***do***, but ***under which conditions of production that they are working***. He does not differentiate different strata in the capitalist class and the working class. The group he calls the middle class, includes both workers who perform capital functions and the petty bourgeoisie.

6.2 The empirical investigation

The Swedish Central Statistical Office, SCB, is not tasked with producing statistics to make a Marxist class analysis. I have chosen to do so based on SCB's statistics 'Enterprises and employees (FDB) by industry ‘SNI 2007, size class, table content in 2011' (SCB 2017-07-09). 2011 is the last year they have collected these statistics. For 2016, there is only the number of companies, not the number of employees. Until company-level data is available, it still requires many assumptions.

6.3 Methodology

About 75,000 data records was manually entered into a 550 x 900 matrix. This is some 5,690,000 people (out of a population of 10 million).

I have excluded one person of each company as the owner, so as not to overestimate the number of employees. In some cases, it is of course an employed person who perform the ownership function. This gives a certain, but limited, overestimation of the number of petty bourgeois and capitalists, which we will have to correct later with other analyses.

6.4 Assumptions

95% of the employees in Department I, II, and raw material production constitute the collective worker, i.e. 5% perform market relating and ownership functions.

About 50% of the employees in trade are estimated to be transport and packaging workers, 50% unproductive. Concretely, a person can perform both productive and unproductive functions. Note that the productive work in commercial capital firms is being automated at a rapid rate, and we can expect the pool of productive workers employed by commercial capital to shrink sharply over the next few decades. 95% of paid reproductive work (the rest is unpaid and done by parents, children and other relatives) is done in the public sector and is unproductive. 5% enriches a private capitalist and is productive and distributed between the working class and the market relating and ownership functions in the proportion 95-5% as before.

All employees in the financial sector perform market relating or ownership functions and are unproductive.

6.5 Definitions

Workers

With the help of these statistics, only the 'collective worker' can be categorized. We cannot see how they are stratified because of what capital functions they possibly perform. To proceed further, the larger companies in each industry must be identified. Due to different organic composition, averages are not useful. By identifying the largest companies in each industry, we can study the financial statements of the individual companies and get a better idea about the class structure. The smaller companies usually have a lower organic composition are of less relative importance, and we will therefore get a good idea of the stratification of the working class by studying the large companies.

Capitalists

- ***Small capitalists*** with 10-99 employees.
- ***Medium-sized capitalists*** with 100-499 employees.
- ***Major capitalists*** with more than 500 employees.

Some capitalists own several companies, so this statistic overestimates the number of capitalists. We would get a better idea by analyzing the individual companies.

Petty bourgeoisie

PB 0. These are "moonlight farmers" or equivalent. These are several different categories:

1. Hobbyists who do not want to become entrepreneurs, are trying to cover the costs of pursuing their hobby.
2. Proletarianized petty bourgeois. The company can no longer support them, and they must take up employment to support themselves. They continue to run the company and possibly use part of the salary to invest in the company, to be able to reboot if possible. Or they have not yet been able to liquidate the company, because of debts.
3. Employees trying to establish themselves as petty bourgeois.

PB 1. Proper petty bourgeois. The entrepreneur and his or her family make up the most important part of workforce.

PB II. This group consists of two categories:

1. Those who 'happened' to grow. This category should change significantly over the business cycle.
2. Those who have ambitions to become capitalists.

Many in the category SB II will go back to SB I. Partly because it is difficult to cope with the competition; with employees, you must have a more 'factory', standardized production than the 'fixing' in various professions that characterizes the petty bourgeois. Partly because life as a very small capitalist is often less bearable than for a petty bourgeois. Those who progress and grow must base this on being unique, e.g. based on innovations, to be able to cope with the competition with larger capital. Category 1 is significantly larger than category II.

The collective worker	***Small***	PB 0
	10-99 employees	moonlight' farmers
	Medium-sized	***PB 1***
	100-449 employees	true petty bourgeoisie
	Major	***PB II***
	> 500 employees	growing towards becoming capitalists

Table 4: Definitions used.

6.6 Sweden in the year 2011

15% of employees are employed in small businesses. It often affects their class consciousness, partly because many develop a dependence on the owner and/or are loyal to the owner. In addition, awareness of the working class as a collective is limited, because the group of employees in the company is small.

Of the others, 34% work for small and medium-sized capitalists and organizations and 51% for large ones.

The distribution of the total number of employed people (outside the labor force are mainly pensioners, the unemployed and those staying at home with children) between the departments is shown in figure 18. The arrows show where the results of each department and reproduction go. For example, part of the production in department I goes to department I itself, i.e. machines to produce machines, etc. The actual state apparatus is financed by taxes and is not part of the productive flow. The financial sector's existence is based on deposits and loans to all parts of society and to the state.

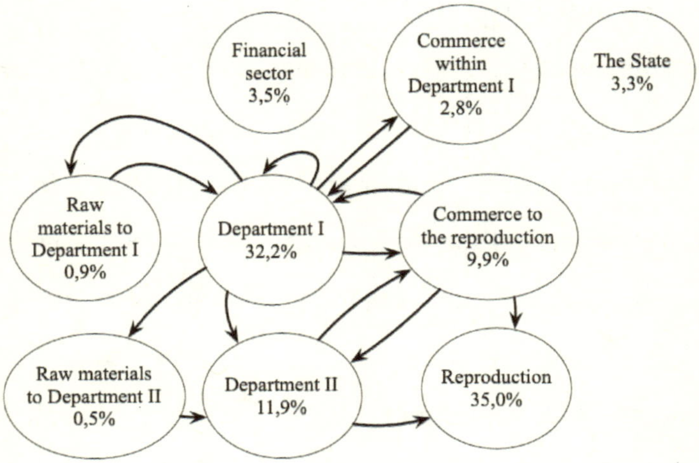

Figure 22. Distribution of the total number of employees between the departments.

65%, of the employment takes place in companies in or connected to department I, which is remarkable and means that a large part of the Swedish capitalist class has no objective interest in bourgeois democracy! (see the discussion above under the section 'capitalism's democratizing and brutalizing forces). This structural distribution explains why Swedish capitalism has weak systemic incentives for democratic reproduction.

Strata	Individuals	Share
The collective worker within Divisions I and II, as well as raw material extraction	1760570	43,2 %
Productive workers in trade	258851	6,4 %
Productive workers in reproduction	71344	1,8 %
Unproductive workers in trade	258851	6,4 %
Unproductive Workers in Divisions I and II and Commodity Extraction	92662	2,3 %
Unproductive workers in the financial sector	140395	3,4 %
Workers in reproduction, neither productive nor unproductive	1355538	33,3 %
The state	135394	3,3 %
Sum	4073604	100,0 %
Workers in reproduction, neither productive nor unproductive		51,3 %

Table 5. Workers and unproductive.

6.7 Political implications of class stratification

Contemporary political discourse in the global North frequently assumes that the working class is shrinking or has lost its centrality.

This chapter has shown that this assumption rests on a misreading of class structure. Even when the analysis is restricted to Marx's strict definition of the working class as productive workers for capital – excluding allied strata in reproduction, coordination, and public services – the working class remains numerically and structurally central.

The perception of decline reflects changes in occupational composition, visibility, and organization, not the disappearance of capitalist class relations. When class is defined by position in the process of value production rather than by cultural markers or employment status, the working class remains the decisive social force in contemporary capitalism. The political question is therefore, not the absence of a working class, but the conditions under which it can recognize itself, organize, and act.

Chapter 6
Contemporary Class Structure, Sweden — Systemic Summary

Sweden demonstrates that, contrary to prevailing claims about a diminishing working class in the 'global North', the working class – defined strictly in Marx's sense as productive workers – continues to constitute a substantial share of the population, even without including allied non-productive strata.

It also shows that a large proportion of Swedish workers are employed in raw-material extraction and Department I industries. Under conditions of declining profitability, this structural position is associated with the growing authoritarian and reactionary tendencies within sections of the Swedish capitalist class.

7. Contemporary Class Struggle

The preceding analysis has direct implications for contemporary class struggle. Workers' leverage does not arise uniformly across capitalism, nor primarily from numerical strength or formal organization. It emerges where production depends on tacit knowing, cumulative learning, and forms of integration that cannot be fully codified, automated, or substituted without loss of value.

Where such tacit knowing is central to production, labor retains a material bargaining position: experience matters, coordination matters, and continuity of the collective worker become economically significant. Under these conditions, capital cannot reproduce value creation independently of workers' active participation.

By contrast, workers are structurally weakest where tasks are modularized, interfaces are fixed, and tacit knowing has been stripped from the work process through standardization or automation. In such settings, competition is governed primarily by price, and labor becomes interchangeable. Contemporary class struggle therefore unfolds unevenly across the value chain, structured by the degree to which tacit knowing remains embedded in production.

7.1 The strategies of the working class and its strata

Reform or revolution

A central problem with the left has historically been the dichotomy “reform–revolution”, i.e., that it is either or. Reformists after Bernstein have argued that it is possible to reform capitalism and thereby achieve socialism (they never mention communism). Revolutionaries after Lenin (also internationalist critics, such as Rosa Luxemburg), have argued that it is necessary to make revolution as soon as possible and that reformism is not a fruitful path.

But neither reformists nor revolutionaries have had any idea of with what ***concretely*** capitalism should be replaced with. Neither had Marx. What we know is only what it should not be characterized by. But this is not a sufficient notion to establish a new social order. And if we see how Marx described the revolutions so far (as when capitalism replaced feudalism, for example), then it is because capitalism developed within the framework of feudal society, but was shackled by feudalism, so that in the end it became necessary to make revolution to develop the full potential of capitalism.

But we see no socialism in the making today: no attempts to build something else. Not even the so-called worker cooperatives differ significantly from ordinary capitalist enterprises. They have neither workers who learn to directly manage the company (instead management is performed by 'elected' directors), nor new mechanisms for cooperation between companies than the market. The conclusion that must be drawn is that within the framework of capitalism, we must push for reforms to improve the workers' position, knowledge, and real influence on all fronts. Only when capitalism's resistance to such changes is strong enough, and at the same time the workers' experience and knowledge are sufficient to take power themselves, can a different society be realized. This was what Marx envisaged – he held that the productive forces must have reached a certain level.

Marx was a politician, but he never developed a political theory, he didn't even finish the economic theory. But according to Marx (Bettelheim 1976; Philipson, 1980), real socialism requires such a development of capitalism that the workers as a collective, not some self-appointed representatives, can rule society.

Trade unionism

Trade unionism is a strategy of protecting the workers, by getting the maximum pay, job security, and protection from accidents. But it does not see any possibility to fundamentally change the conditions of work. It is oriented towards conflict with the individual capitalist, rather than with the capitalist system.

The fight for influence and the workers' councils

In contrast to trade unionism, the fight for influence requires a certain cooperation with the individual capitalist, who will only give up control if there is something for him to gain. The principal reason for such a trade is that the capitalist pursues a value strategy, rather than cost-efficiency strategy. With a value strategy the experience, knowledge, and commitment of the workers has a price.

The fight for influence is not only a "schooling" of the workers for a future "take over", but the actual influence gained reduces the alienation, thus giving energy for further class struggle. The workers understand, individually and collectively, that their experiences are valuable, even compared to the book-knowledge off the engineers and can be transformed to knowledge guiding the work process and eventually to scientific knowledge.

Uniting the collective worker

One of the problems with Kautsky's simplified class theory, is that if you don't see the different interests within the classes, you don't see unity as a problem. But the different interests must be accepted and how to unify the collective worker is a key-issues to be successful in the class struggle.

The role of the wage system in uniting the collective worker

Some workers are “wear and tear” for capital, some are migrants, and many are lone workers, and these always risk falling into separate categories, without influence. When the union at Korsnäs included such workers in a new wage system, with special levels, all in the union fundamentally agreed. The important question of a wage system are the different levels. It is possible to unite the collective worker if it is possible to ascend, to be respected for long and faithful work, and if the differences are “objectively” evaluated. When the bosses have the right to give rewards for unspecified reasons the unity bursts. Individual wages given by the manager is a dividing factor. All workers want the work to function; that the work should give value and lasting results. That is the satisfaction of the work, even when it is monotonous. If you don’t see any value in the work, you become more alienated. A hierarchy that presumes that you only perform based on orders and are neither expected to be able to think, nor to be loyal with the results of the work, is offensive. That is the message in the “rewards for improvement proposals”: ”...if you, you simple devil, finds something that can be improved or even can figure out how it can be done, then we pay for each of your ideas.” The

Korsnäs union could not realize a different system, but wanted the collective, the immediate work unit, to be rewarded collectively., instead of the individual. When you believe that ideas should be rewarded individually, it becomes counterproductive, you withhold ideas. As with variable wages it inhibits effective work. The white-collar workers are expected to think and get nothing extra for a good idea. The logic is that there is a difference between wage earners and salaried employees.

Much of the 1970s focused on "continuous improvements" in many different forms. Capital used many methods and consultancies to drive such improvements. During a short period Korsnäs evolved towards more democracy in the workplace and participation was rewarded. Capital understood the advantage of using "goal management", as it was possible to get everyone to accept the goals as their own. The maintenance workers accepted the objective to do good maintenance work under certain economic restrictions. It demanded a certain reciprocity – that management cared about the conditions of work, the work environment, the wage system, etc. A clear class cooperation at the individual workshop level. When economic controllers changed the goal to be the lowest maintenance costs possible, maintenance workers' motivation was gone.

Organize the collective worker

Marx held that all production workers (up to and including the production manager) were a part of the collective worker (gesamtarbeiter), even if some of them became ideologically deformed, as they performed functions of leading, a part of the functions of capital.

The concept of the 'collective worker' reintroduces the labor process into workplace analysis; by informally working together to resist the iniquities of the labor process, employees collectively become conscious of the conditions of their oppression and exploitation at work. (Lloyd, 2017: 268)

To increase the strength of the collective worker, the blue-collar workers' union at Korsnäs tried to organize many of the workers at the edge of the blue- and white-collar unions, such as laboratory personnel. The union board worked actively to organize the collective worker. The starting point was to prevent various "intellectual" jobs from being absorbed by the white-collar union and supervisor unions. There were two reasons: it reduced the collective strength, and it reduced the knowledge base in the own group.

7.2 Stratified capitalist strategies and alliances

Since long capitalists have deemed capitalism and the free market as a pre-requisite of democracy, while opponents, socialists and anarchist, have agitated that capitalism is the very threat to democracy. This dichotomy is false and unfruitful.

Capitalism has within it both democratizing and brutalizing forces. The very democratizing forces that are necessary to be able to create a higher society beyond capitalism and the brutalizing forces that risk to destroy mankind. The dialectic of this contradiction is playing on all levels of capitalism, economic, politic, and ideologic. This distinction is implicit in Marx's political economy, particularly in his analysis of surplus, rent, and the conditions under which labor becomes merely abstract.

Value-based competition is a democratizing force ***not because capital becomes benevolent***, but because it structurally requires learning, discretion, and worker participation; price-based competition is brutalizing ***not because capital becomes evil***, but because it structurally eliminates those requirements.

I hypothesize that four influences on the political interest of capital:

1. ***Competitive logic (price-based vs value-based).***
2. ***Geography of production vs realization*** *(*where surplus is produced vs sold)

   As discussed in Chapters 2 and 3, capital performs distinct producing, market-relating, owning functions; the political orientation of capital depends on which of these functions dominates its accumulation strategy, and in which geographical and competitive context.
3. ***Degree of generalization of capital functions***

   There are 12 types of generalization of the functions of capital (producing, market relating, and owning.[19] Above, we have discussed some of these. Depending on the capitalist's experience, he knows the mechanisms of capitalism more or less well.
4. ***Position in the social division of labor*** (Department I vs II)

   Capitalists in department II have objective interests of democracy in the marketplace where it is selling and often of dictatorship in markets where they are producing, if they are not the same. This is however overdetermined by

[19] cf. Bettelheim, 1970a, 1970b, 1970c, 1971a, 1971b,1972,1976; Bettelheim, Charrière, & Marchisio, 1968, Philipson, 1980).

his general price- or value-based strategy. Capitalists in department I do not need the luxury of democracy. Unless value-based competition in production requires worker participation, in which case democratic concessions may extend into production itself.

Layer	Department I	Department II
On the target market	Dictatorship	Democracy
On the production market		Dictatorship
Production and selling in the same market		Indeterminate

Table 6. The interests of different layers of the capital depending on department (after Philipson, 1980)

As Granovetter (1985) stated, markets are embedded in social relations. The character of capitalism depends on actions of firms and individuals inhabiting capitalism.

Capitalism has provided millions of consumers with choice; quality instead of undifferentiated commodities and the freedom of quitting an abusive employer, punishable by death under feudalism. The possibility to vote, instead of being ruled by autocrats like Nero, Peter the Great, or Idi Amin Dada.

But capitalism can also mean senseless exploitation of miners in Sierra Leone, LSE (2014-04-05), child-labor in Bangladesh

(Ravallion, & Wodon, 2000), or commercial sexual exploitation of children (Estes, & Weine, 2002); threatening ***human rights***.

Table 6 shows how the immediate economic interests of each stratum depend on their role in the overall production process and where their production and sales take place. In the geography where capital has production, they are interested in low wages and where they have a market for their products and services, they are interested in consumers with purchasing power able to choose their products and services.

Capitalist Stratification and Political Alignment (Three Cases)

In general, it can be said that consumer goods companies have an interest in democracy and good conditions for consumers. and producer goods companies are unconcerned with the plight of consumers and favor a dictatorship. These tendencies are moderated by whether it concerns the companies' producer or sales market. For Apple, the US is mainly an outlet market, although they do have some production there. They therefore have an interest in democracy in the United States, which is showed in the fact that they, together with many other high-tech companies, offered some resistance to Trump – until he became to dangerous. Of course, this does not prevent them from doing everything to avoid taxation in the US; each company is closest to itself. In China, however, Apple's situation is more complicated. It is their crucial production market, with millions of workers at subcontractors. But also, an important sales market. They do not question the Chinese dictatorship (BBC, 2017-05-04; Economic Policy Institute, 2017-05-04). The Koch brothers, on the other hand, with very large interests in the producer goods industry, above all in the USA, have invested in Trump and various right-wing extremist groups (Alternet, 2017-05-09). This also applies to the financial capitalist Mercer, who made his fortune through investment advice to other capitalists. He funded Steve Bannon and his alt-media Breitbart News, he was the backers of the former Vice President Pence and he owns Cambridge Analytics, which used advanced technology to manipulate public opinion before the Brexit vote in England and the election of Trump in the United States (The Guardian, 2017-12 -02). Peter Thiel, the owner of Palantir is the principal backer of the then Vice President Vance, and now the Vice President Vance (Courier International, 2024-11-28).

The capitalist has different objective interests, depending on how he pursues the value production. Unless he needs the active participation by his employees in the production or if he only produces in a given market, for consumption in another market, the interest is to give the workers only baseline wages. But there are plenty of 'idiots' in Department II and the occasional 'decent guy' in Department I. To take a position on possible alliances and dangerous enemies, concrete analyzes of concrete conditions must be made. As is shown in the Korsnäs case below, the individual capitalist can have different interests in different markets and hence pursue different strategies. The strategy can consequently also change, because of changes in the marketplace.

It is common for the left to believe that the various layers of the capitalist class are 'equally good cabbage eaters'. Treating the capitalist class as internally homogeneous is not only analytically wrong, but strategically disastrous:

1. It is a 'leftism', in the sense that it overestimates the progressive forces. In a situation where fascism threatens (Germany in the twenties and early thirties or the United States today) the bourgeois democratic forces are a possible counterforce to fascist capitalism.
2. It is based on a duo-political view of the labor movement's task; where primitive trade unionism, which only interested in improving the reproduction of labor (wages and social conditions) is left to the trade union movement and social democracy. The rest of us must instead realize the revolution. This bifurcation of the labor

> movement was completely foreign to Marx. The task of the labor movement is not only to improve the reproduction of the labor force, but also to strengthen the workers' control of the work. Through such a struggle, workers' understanding of how capitalism works and their ability to take control of certain functions of capital develops. This, together with increased scientific education of the workers, was what Marx means by the development of the productive forces. This development is still minimal for most of the working class. The opportunity to expand workers' control over work is probably generally greater in companies in Department II than in Department I, but generally in companies (whether in department I or II), that pursues a value strategy.

A good description of how the capitalist class can act are the books of Söderpalm (1970, 1976), concerning what happened "behind the scenes" in Sweden in the 1930s and 1940s.
The idea of a non-stratified capitalist class makes it impossible to understand why they react differently, where to attack for success in the struggle and how to fight fascism. A fundamental difference within the capitalist class is that when the profit rate declines (as presently), capital in Department I and raw-material sectors possesses an alternative accumulation strategy – state-financed

militarization – which bypasses market democracy altogether. That was the case in the 1920s, when four of the five principal bank rollers of Hitler were Thyssen, Krupp, Bayer Leverkusen, and IG Farben (Guerin, 1939/1973; Borkin, 1980; Pool, & Pool, 1980). The exception was Henry Ford, an ideologically motivated nazi, who also financed an attempted but abortive coup against President Rosevelt. (The Guardian, 2022-01-11).

7.3 Theoretical deviations within Marxism

Mechanical materialism

None of the main leaders of the surge of the European left in 1968 were economists themselves. They received their knowledge of Marx' theory of economy from works such as Braverman (1974) and Baran & Sweezy (1970), who propagated a fundamental revisionism of Marx, in that they held that capitalism is driven by managerial control, rather than value accumulation: This is the most fundamental revisionism in the history of the left, as it denounces the foundation of Marx: theory of capitalism as explained by the value theory. But they were still claiming to be Marxists, without even discussing how such a revision would explain capitalism and its development. Following Braverman, Marx's theory of the labor process has been widely understood to propose that deskilling is inherent to capitalist management, accomplished via work simplification and mechanization (Vidal, 2019: 171).

Labor Process Theory focused on the dialectic between control and resistance in production, rejecting the then prevailing wisdom that work was becoming more skilled and alienation subsiding (Braverman, 1974). Braverman suggested instead that work was being de-skilled and, that Taylorist 'scientific management' degraded work and made labor power a commodity increasingly cheapened by the capitalist mode of production (Lloyd, 2017: 268) Braverman was right in his disruption of the hitherto views of the evolution of capitalism, ***but not in proposing that this was inevitable***.

The post-modernization of Marxism

Following Berger, & Luckman (1967) and to some extent Foucault (2008) the importance of a concrete analysis of the economy was denied. Society is said to be a social construct, which is correct in the limited sense. Even though these "Marxists" state that the economy is "ultimately determining society", they are not explaining what this is supposed to mean. It legitimizes lofty political and ideological ideas, without any anchoring in the concrete analysis of the economy.

The shift in focus from class, towards identity, was constitutive of the 'cultural turn' of postmodernism and had implications for the sociology of the workplace (Lloyd, 2017: 271). But as my critic of Kautsky above, this more Bernsteinian vision of society as identities cannot be denied, even it is not the ***main*** aspect of society.

Marx developed the most revolutionary theory of the social sciences, but not many of his followers have been adhering to it. From Karl Kautsky, the German communist party leader, up until the first world war, over Lenin, Trotsky, or Mao Tse-tung, as well as those minor leaders of the so called left after 1968, all in some important respect revised Marx theory. These revisions have all been treated as if they are of no consequence to being a Marxist.

7.4 Implications for class strategy

Class struggle is a complex category that has seldom been correctly understood. In figure 23 some of the most important determinations with reference to the chapters and subchapters where they are principally discussed.

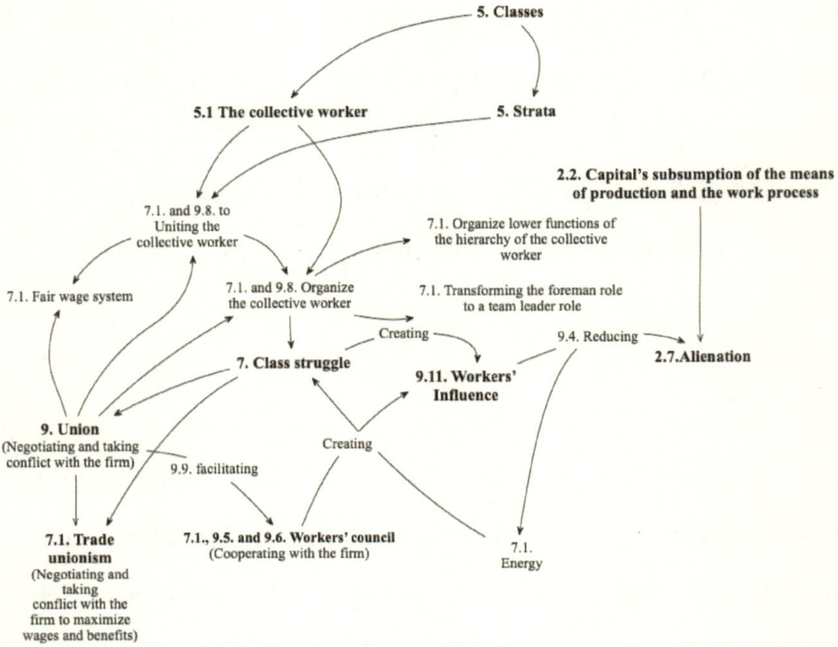

Figure 23. Workers' class struggle.

This shows how systemic tendencies are mediated, how institutions temporarily suspend price-based competition, and how learning and worker influence can emerge.

The following insights becomes politically decisive:

Workers gain leverage where:

- functions are non-substitutable
- learning is cumulative
- integration cannot be automated

Workers are weakest where:

interfaces are fixed

tasks are modularized

price-based competition rules.

Chapter 7
Contemporary Class Struggle — Systemic Summary

Under capitalism, working-class struggle has largely been confined to securing wages necessary for reproduction and to improving immediate working conditions – what is conventionally referred to as trade unionism.

However, the development of workers' collective capabilities requires that class struggle extend beyond wages and conditions to the organization of production, learning, and control over the work process, as well as to the protection of capabilities already achieved.

Capitalist strategies vary according to the position of individual capitals within the system and to the phase of the capitalist cycle. Under these conditions, capital may act either as a democratizing or as a brutalizing force.

8. Economic Democracy in Law: The Swedish Settlement

8.1 The postwar compromise and the legal architecture of economic democracy

After the great strike of 1906, the Swedish trade unions sold out the sole right to manage the work process, to get the employers acceptance of the right to unionize (LO, 2022-06-26). The objective was to influence pay, worker security, and to a limited extent job security. In 1938, this was enshrined in the Saltsjöbaden agreement between the Landsorganisationen, the national labor union, and the organization of employers' organizations. The Swedish trade unions, with few exceptions, limited their role to classical trade unionism, selling labor power collectively to a negotiated price and to work with labor safety.

Trade unionism, to try to get the maximum pay or reducing working time are incompatible with building influence. The company is not interested in cooperating with a union that in each situation tries to get the maximum short-term benefits. An extreme example is the harbor workers in Gothenburg, who managed to acquire salaries of 50.000 SEK per month (some 4500 € per month) for, in reality, a 30 hours work week, equivalent to 2,5 times more than most Swedish workers. This increases the costs for those firms that use the harbor, indirectly putting pressure on the workers in those firms. But the "left" would always support fighting unions, even if their struggle was strictly one of self-interest.

The political discussion concerning economic democracy[20]

In the 1970s and 1980s both the Swedish social democratic and liberal parties had extensive mainly internal discussions on "economic democracy". The discussion in the Social Democratic Party was driven by Landsorganisationen, LO, the main blue collar workers' union. An internal LO project under the leadership of Rudolf Meidner, presented a proposal for "Löntagarfonder" (employee funds) at the union's congress in 1976. With such funds a certain percentage of the private companies' profits should be transferred to funds controlled by the unions. It was estimated that all major companies would be owned by such funds after some 30 years. This was much to the chagrin of the social democratic party leadership. It took seven years for them to dismantle its revolutionary potential. In the finally accepted version, the funds were state and not union owned, limited in scope, could only own 8% of any company. and would be used give companies risk capital. (Klas Eklund, 2023-01-18)

---

[20] For the societal and legal background, I interviewed Klas Eklund (2023-01-18), the then right hand of the Swedish Social Democratic finance minister, Kjell-Olof Feldt and Bengt Westerberg (2023-04-24), liberal (then named "Folkpartiet") party leader in the 1980s and 1990s, and my boss at the ministry of industry 1978-1979.

In 1991, after the bourgeoise parties gained the elections, these funds were dismantled and the funds were partly given finance research at universities. The discussions in the liberal party were oriented towards "shareholder democracy", giving employees shares individually in the company in which they worked. (Bengt Westerberg, 2023-04-24) In the bourgeois government there was not even room for the individual shareholder democracy proposed by the liberals who were part of the government.

8.2 The co-determination act (MBL)

In 1976 a co-determination law [Medbestämmandelagen] was implemented by the then social democratic government. At the same time a law on the position of trade union representative [Lagen om facklig förtroendeman] was taken, which gave union representatives paid leave for union work (LO, 2022-06-26), both laws was giving hopes for real influence at the workplace. However, with few exceptions this proved to be optimistic. The workers came to call the law "the horn" [Tutan]; the company only had to sound the horn, by informing about planned changes, start negations, immediately finishing them, finding that the parties could not agree. Then the company was free to proceed with its plans.

The law gave the unions formal rights to information, negotiation, and influence over reorganization.

8.3 Economic democracy as influence, not ownership

Swedish debates on economic democracy departed in an important way from both orthodox social democracy and revolutionary Marxism. Rather than focusing on the immediate transfer of ownership, reformers concentrated on the question of influence: influence over work organization, production planning, capabilities development, and – indirectly – investment decisions.

This orientation reflected a pragmatic reading of capitalist constraints. Ownership of capital, as Marx emphasized, concentrates decisive power over allocation and accumulation. Yet Swedish reformers recognized that direct ownership transfer was neither politically feasible, nor sufficient to secure workers' emancipation. Without the capabilities required to organize and govern production, formal ownership would amount to little more than legal title.

Economic democracy was therefore conceived as a process rather than an event. Influence was to be built gradually within capitalism, through institutionalized participation in decisions shaping the labor process and the conditions of value creation.

Laws such as the co-determination act (MBL) were designed to open spaces where workers could intervene in managerial decisions – not as co-owners, but as collective bearers of productive knowledge.

In this sense, Swedish economic democracy aimed at transforming the internal relations of production before transforming property relations. It treated ownership not as a starting point, but as a possible outcome of a longer process of learning, capability formation, and institutional struggle.

8.4 The missing condition: learning and capability

The Swedish model assumed that legal rights would translate into effective influence. Experience showed that this assumption was only partially valid. While MBL created formal access to information and consultation, it did not in itself generate the capacities required to use those rights effectively.

What was missing was a systematic strategy for learning.

Where economic democracy made progress – as in Korsnäs – it was not because of the law alone, but because legal rights were combined with organized learning processes: study circles, union education, and the accumulation of workplace-specific knowledge. These practices allowed workers to interpret information, formulate alternatives, and intervene credibly in discussions about production, quality, and investment.

This highlights a crucial distinction: the transition from legal right to effective power is not automatic. It depends on the development of collective capabilities. Without such capabilities, participation risks becoming formalistic, reduced to ritual consultation or defensive negotiation.

Learning, in this context, is not an individual cognitive process, but a material and social one. It takes place through participation in production, interaction with engineers and managers, and collective reflection on the labor process. Economic democracy therefore presupposes institutions that stabilize and protect learning over time.

The absence of a generalized strategy for capability formation helps explain why economic democracy advanced unevenly, even within a favorable legal framework.

8.5 The political defeat of economic democracy

The stagnation of economic democracy in Sweden was not the result of technical flaws or legal impossibility. It was the outcome of political and economic counter-mobilization.

Employers adapted quickly. Where participation threatened managerial prerogatives, they responded by reorganizing production, centralizing decision-making, outsourcing, and intensifying price-based competition. These strategies reduced the relevance of workplace knowledge and undermined the material basis for worker influence.

At the same time, the broader ideological climate shifted. The rise of shareholder value, financialization, and internationalized competition reframed firms as assets to be optimized rather than productive organizations to be governed. Under these conditions, participation was redefined as inefficiency and learning as costs.

The result was a paradox: the legal framework of economic democracy largely survived, but its substance was hollowed out. MBL remained in force, yet the conditions under which it could be used to build influence eroded. Law without supportive economic and organizational conditions proved insufficient.

This outcome illustrates a central theme of this book: rights that are not anchored in material capabilities and protected against competitive pressures become symbolic rather than transformative.

8.6 Why Sweden matters theoretically

The Swedish experience occupies a unique theoretical position.

First, it demonstrates that economic democracy is legally and institutionally feasible within capitalism. The question is not whether participation can be formalized, but under what conditions it becomes effective.

Second, it shows that failure was not technical, but political and economic. The problem was not that workers' influence was impossible, but that it was insufficiently defended against price-based competition, employer strategies, and ideological shifts.

Third, the Swedish case refutes two dominant Marxist misreadings. Against Leninist substitution, it shows that worker capability and influence cannot be imposed from above by party or state. Against accelerationist theories, it demonstrates that capitalist collapse does not automatically generate emancipatory outcomes.

Instead, the Swedish experience supports a third position: transition depends on the temporally extended development of workers' capabilities within capitalism, under conditions that partially suspend its most brutalizing tendencies.

In this sense, Sweden provides neither a model to be copied, nor a failure to be dismissed. It offers a concrete historical laboratory for understanding how class struggle, learning, and institutional design interact – and why the question of transition must be framed in terms of temporality, not rupture alone.

Chapter 8
Economic Democracy in Law: The Swedish Settlement
— Systemic Summary

In Sweden during the 1980s and 1990s, workers' influence was explicitly debated in terms of extending control over the functions of capital.

Resistance from capital, supported by the Social Democratic government, drew a firm boundary at ownership, while effective influence over market-relating and producing functions was only weakly institutionalized.

The resulting framework provided workers primarily with rights to information and consultation, rather than with decision-making power. As a result, workers' influence remained contingent and fragile, dependent on organizational strength and learning rather than secured through law.

9. Value-Based Competition in Practice: The Korsnäs Case

The Korsnäs paper mill was in the 1980s and 1990s the largest paper mill in Sweden, owned by Jan Stenbeck, a dynamic entrepreneur, who had inherited the company, but who independently had created Comvik and Tele 2, two companies that together was the second telecom operator in Sweden.

The Korsnäs case is analyzed as a concrete instance of how value-based competition temporarily suspends capitalism's price logic, allowing workers to acquire capabilities and influence over the producing and market-relating functions of capital. The Korsnäs case is analyzed not as an exception, but as a temporally bounded interruption of capitalism's dominant competitive logic. It is presented here not as a model to be replicated, but as a historically specific demonstration that worker capability formation within capitalism is possible under determinate conditions.

The chapter traces (1) how this window was opened, (2) how learning and influence accumulated, and (3) why it closed.

9.1 Method and data collection

This is a case study (Yin, 1994) which uses multiple data collection methods (Eisenhardt, 1989). The paper is based on lengthy unstructured interviews with three of the four leading labor leaders at the Korsnäs paper mill, during the studied period: Åke Lamm (2020-01-15; 2020-03-04), the union leader, Ulf Westin (2020-10-02; 2020-11-23), member of the union board and Joe Gibbs (2020-11-04). A fourth person central to the case had unfortunately died. The interviews were transcribed and sent to the interviewees for validation.

The study also has elements of participation, as I was consultant to the union when the company decided to close the filial mill Marma. My role as consultant provided access to internal processes normally invisible to researchers, while interviews and validation mitigated bias.

I also participated as lecturer at a few of the meetings of the “dig where you are”-circles that were formative in building the leadership of the of the future workers’ council. Action research is an iterative process involving researchers and practitioners acting together on a particular cycle of activities, including problem diagnosis, action intervention and reflective learning (Avison, Lau, Myers, & Nielsen, 1999).

This case is not a representative but theoretically revealing.

9.2 The genesis of the Korsnäs council: study circles and alliance building

In the beginning of the 1980s a few militants from the 1968 generation were the left opposition in the labor union at the Korsnäs mill. They were some former members of the then defunct Förbundet Kommunist (FK), a Leninist group, some members of the KFMLr and KFML, two Stalinist groups, and some independent social democrats. The former members of FK had at the time become members of the social democratic or the left parties. The old members of Förbundet Kommunist initiated a study circle based on the ideas in a then popular guide on how to understand your position in society and take actions, "dig where you are" (Lindqvist, 1978). Three years of almost weekly sessions formed a group of a dozen militants that tried to understand why of the working conditions at the mill and how to improve them. I participated twice in these study sessions. The study circles functioned as proto institutions of worker governance, rather than as ideological forums.

Apart from the Åke Lamm and Joe Gibbs, former members of FK, it was only one organized worker, the others were unorganized workers from the shop floor. The objective was primarily defensive; what to expect from the company in the near future.

They often invited engineers to answer questions on how the different parts of the mill functioned. Many of these engineers had worked as workers in the mill or other mills, before or during their education and they were happy that the workers were interested.

Apart from schooling of the participants, the workers gained respect and relations by inviting them. Even the general production manager took part in one of the meetings. By inviting bearers of functions of capital to the circle, they built alliances, which later proved to be useful.

The paper union was an industrial union and not a trade union. The left opposition challenged the social democratic leadership of the union. Lamm became member of the board of the paper union. As such he was an outcast. The chairman was a social democrat, who were fiercely anti-communist, using as much "democratic centralism" as ever Lenin. The board members were in the past 32 years all handpicked by the chairman. He tried to get Åke excluded from the social democratic party, but the workers wrote a text to support Åke Lamm. It was eventually signed by 900 of the 1500 eligible workers and published in the local journal. It was proposed that Lamm should challenge the old union boss. Åke got 64% of the votes. At a mass meeting, where the result was announced, the old union boss scolded the workers for having elected a communist. He was booed at and left. The conflict meant that some on the old board left and some new members became elected. The national paper workers' union tried to question the election but failed. Thus, with some luck a new union board leadership with three members, who had been part of the previous study circle, was elected. This was the precondition for building a workers' influence at the workplace. This organizational struggle was built legitimacy-building, mass support and resulted in breaking "democratic centralism" inside the union.

By inviting and discussing with the engineers and by giving them information, they became allied and did not see themselves as antagonistic to cause of the workers.

Another important precondition was the organizing principles of the paper union, which was that all workers at the company were part of the same union, irrespective of if they were paper machine workers, mechanics, or transportation workers. This facilitated the uniting the collective worker.

Two other paper mills in the region had individual left union leaders, but only at the Korsnäs mill they achieved a critical mass to build the workers' council.

9.3 Stenbeck was a modern capitalist

His strategy for Korsnäs was value-based based competition with focus on quality. To fulfill it he needed workers with capabilities. He wanted the workers to be polyvalent, to understand the market conditions for the paper and understand the quality the customers wanted. If possible, he would have wanted that the same worker could run the machine and maintain it. Such a worker would care about the machine. Stenbeck did not empower workers; his value-based strategy created structural dependence on worker capabilities, which the workers organized to exploit.

Thus, he wanted the workers' to be relative less alienated than in most other firms. This was an advantage for the union in building the council and gaining influence for the workers. At the same time, he perused a price-based at his two telecom companies Comvik and Tele2.

9.4 Building strength – reduced alienation and the energy to fight for more influence

By building the workers' council, it was possible to gain influence on most levels of producing, but in some cases also the market relating function of capital. Examples of the latter was to have workers' representatives in the project team for buying a new paper machine or having worker representatives giving quality requirements for a new engineer with position in the command hierarchy, should have. This shows why Øversveen (2022) is locked into a mechanical materialist understanding of an alienation that can never but increase under capitalism:

> "*...an increasing divergence between humanity's objective potentiality on the one hand and our abilities to control and utilize this potential on the other.*" (Øversveen, 2022: 16).

Less alienation is not pacification; instead, it gives workers greater strategic agency.

9.5 Strategic orientation: Why cooperation was rational under value-based competition

Trade unionism and building influence are often incompatible
As discussed earlier, trade unionism is focused on the reproductive rights of the workers, aggressively fighting the

individual capitalist, rather than cooperating with the individual capitalist with the objective to fight the capitalist system. This foci on e.g. maximizing the wages are often in direct conflict with what is needed to get some influence in the work process. Hence, trade unionism is almost always contradictory to gaining such influence.

This is not an argument against unions, but against reducing class struggle to wage defense alone.

The most alienated and less educated workers are often working alone, with heavy physical work. They are seeking strength in the collectivity of the union but are are not driving the question of influence in the workplace.

9.6 Institutional lever: Using MBL to build representation

Concatenation of time

The workers' council was built by creatively using the new law, MBL for institutional hacking The law required the companies to inform of changes with implications for the workers, such as the appointment of a new manager in the production hierarchy or the investment in a new machine. It also gave the union a certain amount of time for education. According to the law, a certain number of hours per worker and year was at the disposition of the union. These hours could be concatenated and used as the union decided. In the Korsnäs case, the equivalent of almost three full-time workers.

MBL allowed the temporal concentration of legally dispersed rights into organizational power.

Unit-level representatives

Rather than themselves becoming full-time representatives, the board used the union time to organize meetings at the level of the units and let the workers in the unit select a representative. Thus, the law, and that the board members did not intend to profit from it, was instrumental in creating the workers' council.

Embedding representatives in projects

If the company informed that it would invest in a new machine, the union said it had two knowledgeable workers in the concerned department that they wanted to be part of the project. Previously when the company would have informed the union about the investment in a new machine, the union board would have given their opinion, and it would have ended there. The new board told the company that the workers concerned would give their opinion. This altered the market-relating function.

Legitimacy through contribution

As the company know that they would get no fuss if complying, they accepted this. In small steps the company also understood that these workers had knowledge that were valuable. The company learned that the workers could actually contribute. The modification of the project strengthened the morals of the workers and partly diminished their alienation. They company learned to see the value in such workers' participation and the participation in all kinds of projects concerning the producing function of capital was generalized.

Each team selected a safety representative and a team representative. Regularly team meetings were held with these representatives. The next level was, e.g., all the teams on paper machine number 5. When the manager for that machine needed to inform, he knows that if he informed the two workers' representatives for that level and the safety representative and wrote a protocol, he got the information out, did not have any trouble with the workers and had fulfilled his duty of informing. Gradually, the company came to accept the workers' council – without understanding its strategic importance. In 1996, 176 workers were in the council structure out of 1400 [12,6%] organized workers at the time. 99,8% of the workers were organized in the union.

Without the MBL law this would have been immensely more difficult, as the workers, who did not necessarily yet see the benefits of the organization, would have had to put in their own time.

Sixth shift team enabling learning

By agreeing to have a sixth shift team, it was possible for workers to go beside someone else to learn a new job, cover for someone who was sick, or to be away for education on union time. This agreement was possible because the paper mill is a capital-intensive business, the cost of the workers is much less important than the cost of a machine that is not running.

9.7 The union newspaper as organizational infrastructure

Another important part of building the organizational infrastructure and confidence was the union journal, Karskäringen, which they published every 6 to 8 weeks. Through the direct contact between the board and the workers trough the council and through their contact with company management and the company board, the paper became the best information provider at the company. And the information was brought out to everybody. It was recognized even by the company; after a few years the union had 60 managers that subscribed to the union paper. It countered the hegemonic information system of the firm.

9.8 Uniting the collective worker

To get strength, the union needed to unite the workers, despite their different interests, whether it was because they were marginal in the process (as those driving a forklift truck) or essential experienced workers running one of the paper machines. The latter was highly respected and well paid. To unite the workers, it was essential to get a pay and promotion system that seemed fair and accessible for all. That eliminated favoritism from the foreman and allowed everyone that wanted to access the education necessary, to make a "career" in the workforce. The union managed to get the company to agree to such a new system. This was boundary work against capital's divide-and-rule. It is also a precondition for workers' capability development.

Organizational boundary work

Strength presupposes that as much of the collective worker as possible is organized. The union took the initiative to organize all the laboratory technicians, hitherto only organized in the blue-collar union at the third paper machine. Although they were part of the production, they would otherwise have been organized in the white-color union. It was more difficult was to organize the cleaners, but they successfully managed this, giving the cleaners a substantial increase in pay. By replacing the foremen, who usually have a union of their own, with team leaders, this first level of the hierarchy was reclaimed for the workers.

9.9 The relation between the workers' council and the union

Lenin and Trotsky did not accept that either the union or the soviet had any influence in managing production. For Shliapnikov it was the union that should control production and for many of the independent workers it was the soviets.

Korsnäs had another solution, working with both, giving them different roles. The council was an organization of cooperation with the company, participating in project groups for exploring a new machine or a new work organization. It was not in conflict with the company and worked to increase the value of the company's products. Although it was hence an organization for cooperating with the capitalist, it foreboded a future where it would take control. It helped workers to gain knowledge on how to run the overall production process, what was important in achieving product quality and how their experience, their tacit knowledge might become important for improvements. Cooperation was tactical, conditional, and subordinate to capability formation. It was built for learning and government.

The union arbitrated conflict when the council could participate, when agreements had to be made with the company and when conflicts had to be taken to protect the workers.

This is a dual-institution solution to the Leninist impasse.

9.10 Tacit knowing as value: The wood-chip moisture example

Once Åke saw a worker, having what was considered the most menial task at the mill, to load the paper machines with wood chips. He mixed chips from different stacks when loading. Åke asked why and the worker said that the level of moisture in the different stacks probably affected the quality of the pulp at the end of the process. Åke connected him with one of the engineers, who gave the worker access to real-time quality information of the pulp, allowing the worker to consciously manipulate the quality of the finished pulp. The moisture control increased the quality of the pulp and hence customer value, which gave the company rents.

9.11 Influence achieved over two functions of capital

The influence gained was over two of the functions of capital, producing and market relating.

Several elements of ***producing*** function were influenced: education of the workers, the use of the workers' tacit knowing, a salary system deemed "fair", a small subsumption of the work organization, by substituting foremen with team leaders that were part of the collective and even organizing some of the foremen. The union was adamant that these team leaders should only have limited surplus pay to keep their loyalty with and the collective's trust, while the company wanted to pay substantially more to bring them closer to the employer. As long as they kept their strength, the council managed to keep the wage increase limited. This was a reclaiming of historical roles. In early capitalism before the total subsumption of the work process by capital, senior workers were "masters", actually running the process.[21]

Less influence was gained over capital's ***market relating*** function, which is comprehensible as it is more important for capital to have absolute control over. But for some issues there were still progress made: by specifying the requirements (the job description) for engineers in production and the choice of the engineer chosen. The market relations to the labor market were influenced and by being in the project group for the investment of

[21] The French term for production manager was contre-maître, the master against the masters.

new machines, influence over the market for buying production equipment was influenced.

Producing	Market-relating
New wage system	Buying a new machine
Shop floor layout	Hiring a new engineer
Team-leaders instead of foremen	
Uniting the collective worker by blue-collar unionizing of border categories	

Table 7. Examples of influence.

9.12 The breakdown: When the competitive logic shifts

Market shift: contracting market → cost logic

The market for high-quality carton gradually shifted from value-based to price-based competition. Thus, workers' participation became gradually less relevant for the company.

Bureaucratization via ISO

Even the implementation of the quality standards ISO led to more alienation. ISO as a formal standard, which allows procedural flexibility, compatible with learning and discretion. ISO as such does not require bureaucratic rule-following; its bureaucratic implementation at Korsnäs reflected the broader shift toward price-based competition and cost-centered managerial control. It was implemented by newly examined engineers directly from university, who used a rule book bureaucracy and did not consult the workers.

Ownership/leadership shift: Stenbeck's death and managerialization

It conceded with the death of Mr. Stenbeck, the capitalist controlling the company, while it might be because his children did not have any business experience and thus had to hire managers to even perform the owning functions of capital. It might also have been because the marketplace had entered a different logic, were satisfying demanding customers with superior products was no longer possible and that it was necessary to pursue a logic based on economics of scale to survive in the market.

Internal managerial ideology: Cost-cutting without value calculus

When the economists became more important than the engineers in running the production, the organization was slimmed and there was less time for education, for union time, and the job became more stressful. They started by destructing the unity of the collective worker, by outsourcing maintenance, internal transports, and cleaning. The company's decision was stupid, as it made the business riskier, while saving limited costs. This is the result of a capitalist ideology that does not understand the profit calculus; to diminish costs, without understanding the effects on the value delivered to customers.

Bureaucratization by ISO 9000

Even the implementation of the quality standards ISO 9000 led to more alienation, as it was implemented by newly examined engineers directly from university, who used a rule book bureaucracy and did not consult the workers.

9.13 Internal political fragility: Co-optation and leadership shift

Stenbeck wanted Åke to become personnel director. He refused, but accepted to be employed by the personnel department, but without responsibility to negotiate for the company. However, Stenbeck managed to buy over two other activists, who accepted to represent the company in negotiations.

Because of the organizational fragility of the activist leadership the union around the same time got a new chairman, a traditional trade unionist social democrat. He did not understand that, unless a strike or some open struggle was needed, you must cooperate with the company to achieve anything. Unless you gave the company a margin of error, and tried to achieve changes together, you had ***no*** influence at all. The union wanted to fight to the bitter end and was no longer trusted by the company for cooperative solutions. Although this seems to confirm a so-called leftist position in the class struggle it did nothing to improve the workers' conditions. The company could comply with the law by informing, having a formal recorded negotiation and another one 14 days later, then they were free to do what they wanted. And they did. When they found no ***value*** in cooperating with the union, the did not cooperate. It was a simple as that. This is almost contrary to the analysis of Vidal 2018: 181-182):

> *"Even where workers gain increased participation, discretion, or voice, these arrangements are typically initiated by management in response to crisis or competitive pressure, and they remain subordinate to capital's control over investment and strategic decision-making."*

While Vidal (2019) interprets worker participation as largely confined to defensive situations under capitalism, the present analysis suggests almost the opposite: durable influence emerges only when capital is not under immediate cost pressure, but instead depends on workers' cumulative knowledge, coordination, and learning. Under such conditions, influence is not a concession but a structural necessity.

I hold that when the capitalist is on an expanding market and has the objective to differentiate his products, he is interested in help in building value, while if he is on a contracting market and fighting for the survival of the company, he is not interested in listening. With his two telecom companies Tele 2 and Comvik, he pursued at the same time a price-based strategy.

Some of the council structures are still in place, depending on the workers at each machine. They still have influence on the local leading and on some of the administrating functions, such as the criteria for a new engineer or the ultimate choice of such, or the choice of a new equipment.

9.14 Unrealized ambitions

Two major ambitions were not achieved. The council wanted to get in place a ***collective*** award system for innovations, rather than the individual one that the company had installed. Most proposals are based on more or less ***collective knowledge***, and the workers don’t want to profit from this to get an individual award. Thus, few innovations are proposed. With a collective award system there is no inhabitation to propose it, as the team will get the reward. The worker giving the proposal should be recognized by the company and will also be given recognition by his teammates, as they all profit from it.

They also wanted to launch experiments ***to hire teams***, rather than individuals. This could have given the union a collective ***bargaining power***, as representative of a in the work process organized team, as was often the case in the transition from feudalism to capitalism (cf. Kugelberg, 1970s and others[22]).

There would both have been threshold innovations and would have qualitatively shifted power. In both cases the ambitions were not realized because the window of value-based competition closed.

9.16 Conclusions of the Korsnäs case

What explains the loss of influence? – Objectively and subjectively

The loss of influence was obviously a result of booth objective and subjective circumstances. Objective because of the death of Stenbeck (not necessarily because his death), Korsnäs changed

---

[22] See analyses of collective selling of labour in Swedish ports and construction in Arkiv för studier i arbetarrörelsens historia, mid–late 1970s (e.g. contributions by P. Kugelberg and colleagues. These articles were never digitized or even indexed. Here they are taken from memory.

strategy, from being a high-quality value adder (value-based competition) to cost-rationalization in a decreasing market (price-based competition).

Subjective, because the changes in union leadership were crucial in the development.

What explains the lack of resilience?

The leadership was not broad enough, depending to much on individuals. One of the problems seems to have been that the study circle was seen as a part of building the council, but it was abandoned when the council was in place. Thus, the team that led the building of the council was not broadened by the schooling of new workers. When the leaders transitioned to other tasks in the company or in the broader local political environment, there were not enough schooled leaders left.

A local and national, avant-garde movement was absent. Such a movement could have backed up and supported the union and the council at Korsnäs.

What the case shows

The case demonstrates that capitalism's systemic tendency toward price-based competition can be temporarily interrupted, allowing worker capability formation – but only under specific competitive and institutional conditions. An influence that makes the workers proud of their work and give them a sense of less alienation. The workers realize that they could manage many important decisions of the firm and for some it might have raised the idea that they could potentially collectively run the firm. Such influence can only be built under value-based competition. Even though such influence can only be built under the temporarily of value-based competition, it can survive until a new window of opportunity if learning is institutionalized. Breakdown of value-competition does not erase achieved learning.

Whether these experiences could be generalized, we don't know. A militant workers' movement must make the attempt. Until then any social revolution without such workers' experiences will produce a dictatorship over the proletariat, not a dictatorship of the proletariat.

The Korsnäs case demonstrates that learning is a material process, embedded in the organization of production and in the competitive strategy pursued by capital. During the period in which Korsnäs operated under value-based competition, workers' knowledge, coordination, and tacit skills became productive resources rather than residual attributes. This created a space in which worker capability formation was not only possible, but functional for capital itself.

This space proved fragile. When market conditions shifted and price-based competition became dominant, the organizational conditions that had supported learning and participation were progressively dismantled. Capability formation slowed, and some of the institutional supports for worker influence were withdrawn. Yet many of the effects of the earlier period did not disappear. Even decades after the shift in competitive logic, elements of the knowledge, practices, and organizational confidence developed during the value-based phase remained present among parts of the workforce. This persistence illustrates why temporality matters: value-based competition need not be permanent to be politically and organizationally consequential. Temporarily stabilized learning regimes can leave durable traces, even when the conditions that produced them are no longer intact.

The Korsnäs case shows that worker capability formation is not an epiphenomenon of goodwill or ideology, but a structurally conditioned process that emerges only under specific competitive regimes and temporal protections.

Chapter 9
Value-Based Competition in Practice: The Korsnäs Case — Systemic Summary

The Korsnäs case demonstrates that workers can, under capitalism, develop collective competences in production and coordination when value-based competition makes their knowledge indispensable.

It also shows that such gains can be partially institutionalized and survive beyond the period in which they were created, but remain fragile and reversible once competitive conditions shift back toward price-based competition.

10. Capitalism as a Historical Process

Capitalism does not exist as an abstract model. It exists historically, and therefore always through mediation. The systemic tendencies Marx reconstructed – competition through price, profit-rate pressures, centralization and concentration – operate through concrete institutional forms: labor law, collective bargaining, industrial policy, standards, procurement rules, corporate governance, and antitrust. These institutions do not abolish capitalism. But they can, for extended periods, suspend its dominant competitive discipline and thereby open space for alternative competitive regimes.

This is the first key step toward a non-mechanical reading of Marx. Capitalism contains long-run tendencies, but their historical expression depends on institutional countertendencies. To analyze capitalism dialectically is therefore to analyze the interaction between systemic pressures and the historically specific institutions that channel them.

10.1 Institutions as counter-tendencies

Institutional mediation is not an external "add-on" to capitalism; it is how capitalist reproduction is stabilized. Collective bargaining can raise wages and reduce turnover, but it can also stabilize skill formation and protect the continuity of experience in the labor process. Co-determination and workplace representation can constrain arbitrary managerial control and preserve tacit knowing in production. Standards can stabilize quality competition by making reliability and performance visible and enforceable. Procurement rules can privilege long-term capability, learning, and system integrity, rather than lowest short-term price. Antitrust can block tipping dynamics and prevent infrastructural dominance. Industrial policy can create protected spaces, in which firms compete through learning rather than through cost destruction.

The point is not that institutions "moralize" capitalism. The point is that they can alter the form of competition. When institutions protect learning, continuity, and capability development, they can temporarily weaken the dominance of price-based competition and allow value-based rivalry to persist. When those institutions are weakened – through deregulation, privatization, anti-union strategies, and narrow price-only competition policy – price-based competition reasserts itself, and the brutalizing forces intensify.

10.2 Capitalism never exists without mediation

Institutions can block price-based competition, protect learning, and stabilize value-based competition through collective bargaining, industrial policy, co-determination, standards, procurement rules, and antitrust regulation and application.

Institutions do not abolish capitalism, but they can suspend its dominant competitive logic for historically meaningful periods.

10.3 Value-based competition as a historical regime

Under certain historical conditions, competition is organized primarily around quality, reliability, innovation, coordination, and knowledge. This is not a utopia and not a departure from capitalism. It is a historically recurring regime, in which firms cannot succeed by lowering price alone because performance is not reducible to price. The competitive advantage of firms in such regimes rests on their ability to develop and integrate capabilities – technical capabilities, coordination, process learning, and the cumulative experience embedded in the collective worker.

This is where Penrose (1959) becomes analytically indispensable. In Penrose, the firm is not an equilibrium "production function," but a historically developing organization. Growth is driven by experience and learning; capabilities are accumulated, recombined, and expanded through use. The firm therefore competes through the development of productive services and organizational knowledge, not merely through price adjustment.

Under value-based competition, the knowledge of the collective worker is not a peripheral input; it is a decisive condition of performance

Yet this regime is structurally fragile. Value-based competition requires time, continuity, and protected learning. It presupposes that firms can invest in training, maintenance, supplier collaboration, process improvement, and innovation without being immediately undercut by destructive price-based competition. It also presupposes institutional support that keeps competition from collapsing into a race to standardization.

In some periods and sectors, firms compete on quality, reliability, innovation, coordination, and knowledge. Such competition presupposes learning, depends on worker capabilities, and requires institutional protection. Penrose's firm is a learning system, which grows through experience and generates value through capability development.

Value-based competition can be historically durable, but it is structurally fragile under renewed price discipline.

Chapter 10.
Capitalism as a Historical Process: Institutions, Mediation, and Competitive Regimes – Systemic Summary

Institutions cannot transcend capitalism, but they can mediate its competitive dynamics by suspending price discipline for extended historical periods.

Such mediation makes value-based competition possible and effective, yet never secure: it remains structurally contingent and vulnerable to renewed price-based restructuring.

11. Class Struggle as Mediation, Not Override

Class struggle does not suspend capitalism by will. It operates through mediation: through institutions, rules, organizational forms, and norms that reshape the labor process and the form of its effects are therefore often indirect. Workers may fight over wages and hours, but also over training, staffing, maintenance time, the pace of work, the right to stop production for safety, the right to participate in process redesign, and the institutionalization of representation. These struggles do not merely redistribute value; they reshape the conditions under which value is produced and the kind of firms and strategies that survive.

This reframes class struggle in a way that reconnects Marx's systemic theory to the problem of transition. If competition is organized primarily through price, then class struggle tends to be confined to defensive resistance: wages, job security, and the mitigation of degradation. If competition is organized through value and learning, class struggle can become a struggle over capabilities, participation, and control – over the gradual subsumption of elements of the labor process by the collective worker. In that sense, class struggle is also a struggle over how competition is organized, not only over distribution.

Class struggle does not suspend capitalism by will. It operates through institutions, rules, organizational forms, and social norms. Its effect is indirect; it reshapes competitive regimes, alters the labor process, and changes what kinds of firms survive.

Class struggle is a struggle over how competition is organized, not only over distribution.

Chapter 11. Class Struggle as Mediation, Not Override – Systemic Summary

Class struggle is a struggle over how competition is organized and mediated, not only over distribution.

12. Learning, Capability, and Temporality

Marx and Engels insisted that workers' emancipation must be their own achievement. That insistence has a material implication: workers must develop the capabilities and experience required to manage production and coordinate the wider system of reproduction. This is not a moral claim; it is a condition of possibility. Without worker capability – technical knowledge, collective knowledge, organizational capabilities, and systemic understanding – any "seizure" substitutes one commanding minority for another and reproduces domination in a new form.

As capitalism has become more complex and technologically sophisticated, the management of capital functions has increasingly required scientific and organizational knowledge. Marx anticipated this development in his analysis of the productive forces, were science, technology, and cooperation appear as material conditions of production.

If the working class is to subsume the functions of capital, it cannot do so through experience alone, nor through formal education detached from production. It must acquire the forms of knowledge through which production is coordinated, evaluated, and transformed. Such knowledge does not arise automatically. It emerges through the social organization of learning, the integration of experience and theory, and struggles over who controls knowledge within the labor process.

This chapter therefore analyzes how human experience is transformed into scientific and organizational knowledge, and under what social and institutional conditions such transformations enable collective capability formation rather than technocratic substitution. Without such collective capability formation, attempts to replace capital functions, result not in workers' self-rule, but in substitution by experts acting in their name.

Through what Mintzberg (1979) called work expansion and enrichment of work content, horizontal and vertical centralization in companies can be reduced. This is related to Marx's concept of formal and real subordination of workers to the means of production and the increase in the level of productive forces under capitalism. Without broad job expansion and job enrichment, capitalism has not developed its full potential; the productive forces have not reached their highest level and a 'revolution', in which the workers (and not self-appointed representatives) can take power, is not possible.

Production is therefore not only the site of exploitation; it is also the principal site of capability formation. Through production, human activity is objectified into external reality, and that reality returns as both an accumulated resource and a constraint. In this sense, learning is not an ideological supplement but a material process: workers develop their capacities by altering the world and being altered by the world they have produced (Øversveen, 2022). The decisive question for transition is thus whether capitalism generates, or allows workers to force it to generate, the conditions under which worker capability can develop into collective capabilities.

12.1 Worker capability as a material condition

The hierarchization of the production

The real subsumption of the production took place in steps.

When technology became more complex, specialists, engineers were needed. These were recruited from the shop floor. The next alienation of the workers was when special schools, the technical high schools were created at the end of the 19th century to educate such engineers. Later, when the level of understanding of mathematics, mathematical statistics, physics, and chemistry increased, these became technical universities. This meant that the engineers did not have own experiences (tacit knowing) of work at the shop floor, instead they were taught ready-made digested explicit knowledge. They came to hold the idea that the workers' knowing was relatively unimportant and uninteresting.

Today high school students are educated to become process and machine-drivers, electricians, etc., creating yet another alienating hierarchical level of loss of control for the unskilled workers, making these more educated workers' knowing alienated from the workers' collective. These four hierarchical levels of the modern factory: unskilled worker, machine/process driver, high-school educated engineer, and university educated engineer, where the latter two don't share the experience of the former two and the former two not the knowledge of the latter two, rigidify the modern factory. Labor must fight for the possibility to break these glass ceilings, by access to education later in life.

Transition presupposes a long-run expansion of the collective worker's capabilities: not only skill at tasks, but capabilities in maintenance, coordination, quality judgement, process control, technological development, and organizational decision-making. These capabilities are unevenly distributed across the collective worker. A romantic focus on the least skilled strata obscures the strategic point: the strata with the deepest technical capabilities and process knowledge are often the strata with the greatest potential leverage for expanding worker influence. This is not elitism; it is a recognition that the labor process contains differentiated knowledge positions, and that control over production requires mastery of the system's technical and organizational core.

Capability formation also implies extension beyond "producing" functions toward "market-relating" functions – procurement, quality requirements, supplier relations, investment decisions – and ultimately raises the question of the "owning" function. At that point, if not earlier, capital's resistance tends to become coercive. This is why the development of worker capability cannot be separated from the development of organizational forms and institutions capable of protecting it.

12.2 Why price-based competition blocks transition

Price-based competition is not merely an economic mechanism; it is a discipline that reorganizes the labor process. It fragments work, accelerates turnover, penalizes training, externalizes knowledge into contractors and supply chains, and rewards strategies that cut precisely those investments through which collective capabilities develop. Under price discipline, even well-intentioned reforms tend to be unstable: the competitive pressure returns in the form of cost-cutting, outsourcing, de-skilling, and re-centralization of control.

As a result, class struggle under price-based competition is pulled back toward defensive terrains – wages and job security – because the institutional and organizational basis of learning is continually undermined. The reproduction of domination is not explained by ideology alone; it is reproduced through the competitive form itself.

Price-based competition fragments work, accelerates turnover, externalizes knowledge, and penalizes learning. It confines class struggle to wages, job security, and defensive resistance.

Price-based competition reproduces domination even under progressive politics.

12.3 Temporality: The missing category in mechanical Marxism

Learning takes time. Capability formation is cumulative, collective, and historically layered. Therefore, transition cannot be instantaneous, and crises do not automatically produce emancipation. A crisis may open political space, but it does not generate capabilities. If anything, intensified price-based competition in crisis tends to destroy the very learning and organizational stability required for workers to develop control.

This makes temporality central. If capitalism contains an inner tendency toward price discipline and concentration, then transition requires extended periods in which that tendency is suspended long enough for labor's capacities to transform through institutions that stabilize value-based competition, through durable organizational forms of worker participation, and through the accumulation of experience in managing production. In your terms: capitalism can only be overcome through temporarily breaking its inner tendencies long enough to change what labor can do.

Learning takes time. Capability formation is cumulative and collective. Transition can therefore not be instantaneous, and crises do not automatically produce emancipation.
What is required are extended periods of suspended price discipline, in the form of durable value-based regimes and institutional continuity.

Capitalism can only be overcome through temporarily breaking its inner tendencies long enough to transform labor's capacities.

12.4 To take control; workers' knowledge and skills need to be developed

The forces of production under capitalism

The forces of production is a measure of the 'modernity' of capitalism: the technological development of machines and other means of production (chemical processes, for example) and the collective worker's use of scientific knowledge and scientific methods. Marx firmly believed that the productive forces must reach such a high level that capitalism becomes a straitjacket for the development of these forces for the working class to be at the door of revolution.

The common understanding of Marx concept forces of production is generally very limited, implying that machinery and automation determine the level of the forces of production.

Marx determination of the forces of production is much wider and more complex.[23] They include (Marx, 1969a; Philipson, 1980: 39, Miller, 1981: 95):

- The objective conditions of production (machinery, automation, raw materials and components).
- The subjective conditions of production (the workers, their scientific knowledge).
- The immediate work organization, i.e. the relations between what is worked on (the raw material and the components), the means of work (the objective means, machinery and

---

23 "*Die gesellschaftlichen Produktivkräfte der Arbeit, oder die Produktivkräfte direkt gesellschaftlicher, vergesellschafteter (gemeinsamer) Arbeit, durch die Kooperation, die Teilung der Arbeit innerhalb des Ateliers, die Anwendung der Maschinerie, und überhaupt die Verwandlung des Produktionsprozesses in bewusste Anwendung der Naturwissenschaft, Mechanik, Chemie etc., für bestimmte Zwecke, Technologie usw., ebenso wie das allem diesen entsprechende Arbeiten auf grosser Stufenleiter usw. (es ist nur diese vergesellschaftete Arbeit, die fähig ist, die allgemeinen Produkte der menschlichen Entwicklung, wie Mathematik etc. auf den unmittelbaren Produktionsprozess anzuwenden wie andrerseits die Entwicklung dieser Wissenschaften eine bestimmte Höhe des materiellen Produktionsprozesses voraussetzt), diese Entwicklung der Produktivkraft der vergesellschafteten Arbeit im Gegensatz zur mehr oder minder isolierten Arbeit der Einzelnen usw. und mit derselben die Anwendung der Wissenschaft, dieses allgemeinen Produkts der gesellschaftlichen Entwicklung auf den unmittelbaren Produktionsprozess, dies alles stellt sich dar als Produktivkraft des Kapitals, nicht als Produktivkraft der Arbeit, oder nur als Produktivkraft der Arbeit, soweit sie mit dem Kapital identisch ist, und jedenfalls nicht als Produktivkraft weder des einzelnen Arbeiters, noch der im Produktionsprozess kombinierten Arbeiter. Die Mystifikation, die im Kapitalverhältnis überhaupt liegt, wird jetzt viel weiter entwickelt, als es bei der nur formellen Subsumtion der Arbeit unter das Kapital der Fall war und sein konnte. Andrerseits tritt hier auch die historische Bedeutung der kapitalistischen Produktion, eben durch die Umwandlung des unmittelbaren Produktionsprozesses selbst und die Entwicklung der gesellschaftlichen Produktivkräfte der Arbeit, erst schlagend hervor (spezifisch hervor).*" (Marx, 1969a: 50)

automation, and the subjective, the workers and their scientific knowledge).

Some mechanical materialists deny that the forces of production include the immediate organization of work, holding that it is illogical to recognize any element based on relations as part of the productive forces (Cohen, 1978, cited in Miller, 1981: 104; Cohen, 1978, cited in Coram, 1989: 214). While criticizing Cohen, both Miller and Coram nonetheless reproduce the same limitation, insofar as they also exclude immediate work organization from the forces of production on the grounds that it is relational. This rests on a false opposition. Immediate work organization is indeed relational, but it is not therefore external to the forces of production. It is not autonomously dynamic, but a ***historically given*** and contested form within the concrete labour process itself, through which productive capacities are realized, constrained, or transformed.

For Marx, capitalism develops the level of the productive forces, eventually becoming advanced enough to permit that capitalism can be transcended. Marx wrote that socialism would only be possible when the forces of production had reached a certain level. It does not seem that these 'Marxist' prophets ever asked themselves what these productive forces were, except complete automation of production, making the workers unnecessary; abolishing capitalism by abolishing the workers.

> *"...Marx counted only* ***and singularly (einzig und allein) on the intellectual development of the working class*** *as it necessarily had to come out of the united action and discussion (Marx, 1972: 57; our emphasis)."* (Chattopadhyay, 2003:2)

> *"...productive forces are a system of subjective (human) and material (means of production) elements that reproduce the active attitude of people to nature, which consists in its material and spiritual development and development of its wealth (values), in the process of which the conditions of human existence are reproduced and the process of man's development is being fulfilled".* (Voit, Tkachenko, & Oleshkevich, 2018:35)

This relationship should be considered not only as interaction between people, who are the main chain link (more precisely, mechanism) of relations in the socio-economic system, but also as the appropriate interaction between social formation and nature. The materialization of these interactions forms a new concept of the technological basis of society (its productive forces) and provides dynamic development of intellectual potential, which, in turn, determines the nature of the technological basis of production through the consistent realization of knowledge and changes in productive relations. (Lyashenko, 2006; after Voit *et al.*, 2018: 35).

The process involves not only the knowledge embodied in the technological equipment, in the productive forces in general, but also living knowledge, whose bearer is the creative initiative activity of each person. (Voit *et al.*, 2018:36).

By altering external reality according to our subjective intentions, needs and desires, we develop our own capabilities and self-understanding. For Marx, production is both an expression of our subjectivity and the chief mechanism through which this subjectivity is developed. Through production, we not only develop ourselves as individual agents, but also enter into and develop our relations to nature and to other people (Øversveen, 2022: 6; Philipson, & Kjellström, 2020)

> *"During production, our activities are fixed into externally existing objects, a process which is referred to as objectification" (Øversveen, 2022: 7).*

> *"Through objectification we… create an objective reality that is simultaneously a reflection of our own existence*

> *and an exterior force that stands outside our direct control and which continually threatens to restrict and dominate our free activity..." (Øversveen, 2022: 7)*

The left must stop romanticizing the unskilled and uneducated worker. It is the most educated workers, who have the greatest potential, e.g. the mechanics at the paper mill, not the truck drivers. It was shown in their leading role in both the French Revolution and the Paris Commune. An expansion of the collective worker's control over (subsumption of) the work process, must involve an expansion to capital functions other than ***producing*** (the internal relations of production) to the relationship to the market (the external conditions of production); ***market relating***. In the long run, such extended control leads to the ***owning*** function also being called into question. But there, if not before, the resistance of the capitalists will become violent.

Few recognize the value of workers' tacit knowing, but it is an essentially issue for the workers' organizations to develop these experiences; to develop experienced-based learning, explicit knowledge anchored in the workers' practice (Dietzgen, 1973). This is essential for developing the knowledge and the skills necessary to subsum the work process and to have something to trade with capital while undermining capital's subsumption – if capital finds that the workers have knowledge essential for the value creation it is more open to trade influence against such knowledge.

This is a summary of theories that have been discussed in more detail in Philipson (2016, 2016, 2019) and Philipson, & Kjellström (2020).

The human being is already from the earliest hour a social animal. Language is acquired by ***internalizing*** the meaning, the common descriptor of the sense that the child has of its proximal world (***1, in Figure 24***). The Individual, the ***ego***, is a social animal, an ***id***, developed within a first community of practice, the ***superego*** (Freud, 1974), by ***internalizing*** (Vygotsky, 1970, 1987, 1993, 1994, 1997a, 1997b, 1998, 1999) the ***community of practice*** of which it is a part (Bourdieu, 1976; Dietzgen, 1973; John-Steiner & Mahn, 1996; Weick & Roberts, 1993; Wenger, 2000), and its ***symbolic representations***.

Sensory cues and the actions of the individual and others in the communities of practice, in which they participate, leads to ***experiences***, nodes in the brain. These nodes are related in labile mental structures, ***synapses***, based on the commonalities between different nodes; be they cognitive, emotional, colors, odors, or all other parts of the memory of the experiences. Cognitively unrelated phenomena can be related by, e.g., a common odor or a color, which years later can make the individual sensing that the two phenomena are related.

The mass of the experiences in all the communities of practice that each individual has participated in, before and concurrently now, constitute their ***tacit knowing*** (Polanyi, 1961, 1962, 1968), or sense (Mahn & John-Steiner, 2002; Polanyi, 1961, 1962, 1968; Wertheimer, Brett, King, Peckler, & Schaef, 1992). Vygotsky called this ***lived experience***. For Vygotsky:

> *"...the learning process was not a solitary exploration by the child of the environment; rather, it was a process of appropriation by the child of the methods of action existent in a given culture. In such an appropriation, a crucial rule is played by symbolic tools – signs, linguistic and mathematical systems, and so on."* (Kozulin, & Presseisen, 1995: 67).

Lived experience is forming the individual and her personality; Vygotsky's concept perezhivanie, often described as ***lived or emotional experience***. Every student is formed by 'the specifics of their past experiences' (Mahn, & John-Steiner, 2002: 49-50). These lived experiences are fundamental to the understanding of individual learning styles and culturally contextualized learning (John-Steiner, & Mahn, 1996: 198)

Emotions are socially constructed and internalized (***1, in Figure 24***). They play a key role in shaping motivation and thought (Levykh, 2008; Mahn, & John-Steiner, 2002). The individual's emotional experience is foundational (consciously, subconsciously, and unconsciously) to the person's perception, attention, memory, decision-making, behavioral mastery, and overall world orientation (Levykh, 2008). Vygotsky believed that affect and intellect are not two mutually exclusive poles, but two inseparable mental functions (Levykh, 2008: 85).

Motivation is the mediation between emotions and thought. Motive gives birth to thought, to the formation of thought itself, to its mediation in internal words, to the meanings of external words, and finally to words themselves (Mahn, & John-Steiner, 2002)

> *"Doodling, drawing, modeling, sketch ideas and make things, and you're likely to encourage accidental discoveries. At the most fundamental level, what we're talking about is play, exploring borders."* (Kelley, 2001: 38)

Such ***boundary objects*** (Boland Jr., & Tenkasi, 1995), within the realm of tacit knowing, are ***thinking sketches***, in the words of Ferguson (1992), where the sketches are used to dialogue with a 'virtual 'other'. This dialogue can provoke semi-conscious and unconscious tacit knowing to surface to higher level of consciousness.

Tacit knowing

Sensory cues evoke mental imagery, based on earlier experience (Holbrook, 1982). This imagery is the essence of the concept tacit knowing. The sense of a word is the aggregate of all psychological facts [Gestalt] that arise in our consciousness, provoked by the word (Wertheimer et al., 1992). Polanyi (1962: 604) is drawing on Gestalt psychology in his attempt to establish the logic of tacit knowing:

> *"Gestalt psychology, on which I am drawing throughout this attempt to establish the logic of tacit knowing..."*

Our spontaneous understanding is phenomenological, descriptive. Sensory-rich and extensive experiences, build tacit knowing with potential to create innovations. Extensive means experiences in many communities of practice, different cultures, and physical environments. Sensory-rich experiences allow a more complex network of synapsis that relates different experiences and makes it possible to retrieve experiences from non-active memory. Tacit knowing includes conscious and unconscious tacit knowing, as well as explicit knowledge, ***embedded*** in and understood within tacit knowing. Conscious tacit knowing. It is not readily communicable, even if the holder wants to communicate it, both because it is embedded in unconscious tacit knowing and because it has yet no, or not enough, shared meaning with those with she wants to communicate with.

Unconscious tacit knowing. It is not accessible for the individual herself. It is not in, what Polanyi (1962) called focal awareness. It must be revoked by means unknown to the individual and it is even more difficult, if not completely impossible, for another person to provoke the making conscious of such knowing (cf. the role of the psychotherapist).

There is no absolute distinction between conscious and unconscious knowing. As the individual's experience grows and deepens, old experiences retreat to the background and new ones take the foreground. Neither is there a garbage can at the end of this displacement, other than dementia. Subdued unconscious knowing can come to the foreground again, provoked by new experiences or tacit inferences to old ones. The distinction between explicit, conscious, and unconscious tacit knowing is therefore fuzzy.

Externalization of tacit knowing

Making explicit is to externalize (Borthick, Jones, & Wakai, 2003). Tacit knowing can partly be transformed to explicit knowledge through externalization (***2, in Figure 24***).

Externalization is made in written or oral language, visualization, and behavior, even with odor, fragrance, scent, and aroma. However, such transformation is always incomplete; we cannot transfer the rich sense of tacit knowing into explicit knowledge, since the latter becomes a mere shadow of the former.

When negotiating meaning within the community of practice, a tool with an understanding of the other (empathy) as a conduit, needs to be constructed; cf. ***talking sketches*** (Ferguson, 1992; Van Der Lugt, 2005), sketches rich enough and accompanied with oral descriptions. The learning within the community of practice is consequential of the quality of the ***dialogue, collaborative sketching***, and ***experimental work*** in the community of practice. The negotiating of meaning normally results in the individual's need to reconcile in her mind the "truce" (Nelson & Winter, 1982) of common meaning of the tacit knowing – or to re-negotiate. In

Philipson, & Kjellström (2020), we were discussing in detail how such visual representations are central in the externalization of tacit knowing.

To negotiate a common meaning in a community of practice in the organization at large, the dialogue takes place over boundary objects (Boland Jr. & Tenkasi, 1995), or talking sketches (Ferguson, 1992; Van Der Lugt, 2005). A series of talking objects are initiated after a member of the group presents her most refined thinking sketch. Boundary objects are at once ***temporal*** (Schalow, 2013), based in action, subject to reflection, and local tailoring in dialogue, and distributed throughout all these dimensions (Star, 2010). To negotiate meaning is a difficult task, facing the designer who wants to interact within their community of practice. To modulate ideas and thoughts, the individual needs to externalize them, objectify them with psychological tools, such as language, symbols, drawings, etc. (Herrenkohl & Guerra, 1998; Herrenkohl, Palincsar, DeWater, & Kawasaki, 1999; Levykh, 2008; Palinscar & Herrenkohl, 2002), by negotiating meaning with oneself; cf. thinking sketches (Ferguson, 1992; Van Der Lugt, 2005). These tools are mediators for the individuals' negotiation of meaning and sense (Mahn, & John-Steiner, 2002), prior to the ***negotiation of meaning*** in a community of practice. To negotiate meaning in a community of practice is to internalize the experiences of others

(***3, in Figure 24***), to get a more objective experience. This negotiated understanding is explicit knowledge.

Talking sketches refer to designers making use of the (shared) drawing surface in support of the group discussion. Talking sketches, spontaneously drawn during discussions with colleagues, will continue to be important in the process of going from vision to artefact.

This process is the negotiating of meaning; it is to be able to express and dialogue around previously individual conscious tacit knowing, but now made explicit knowledge, in a limited community of practice, a team. The characteristics of the team as a community of practice is that it has a very detailed and profound negotiated meaning, developed from a common professional education and common practice. For others in the group, an intervention might provoke a discourse based on explicit or conscious tacit knowing or provoke unconscious tacit knowing to surface to consciousness. This dialogue can develop new knowledge, but the discourse itself is limited by what can be made explicit.

Learning is largely achieved within the social and collaborative processes that involves the development of shared experiences in communities of practice, within which learning takes place (Lam, 2014; Lave & Wenger, 1991; Wenger, 1998). Communities of practice are "…groups of people informally bound together by shared expertise and passion for a joint enterprise." (Wenger & Snyder, 2000: 139). Knowledge and learning are largely only achieved within a community of practice (Borthick *et al.*, 2003; Brown, & Duguid, 1991; Kinginger, 2002; Lave, & Wenger, 1991; Orr, 1996; Vygotsky, 1999; Wenger, 1998).

Talking sketches, and their language equivalents, are ***the mediation between tacit knowing and explicit knowledge***. The essence of the dialogue in this mediation process is problematizing (Alvesson, & Sandberg, 2011); or problem-probing.

External knowledge

Meaning can be viewed as explicit knowledge and sense as tacit knowing. The way we endow our own utterances with meaning and our attribution of meaning to the utterances of others are acts of tacit knowing. They represent sense-giving and sense-reading, within the structure of tacit knowing (Polanyi, 1962). Meaning is only the most stable and precise zone of sense (Mahn, & John-Steiner, 2002).

Knowledge does not reside in the individual's head, but in the communities of practice, in which they participate. The concept of community of practice (Wenger, 2000) indicates a functioning team, with a intentionality of learning together. We suggest that professional teams share a 'conditional intentionality' (Cf. 'conditional trust' proposed in Philipson, & Philipson, 2016). If such conditional intentionality breaks down, learning is no longer possible.

To communicate knowledge outside of the direct community of practice, requires the use a less shared common negotiated meaning, limited by a common culture. Such a dialogue takes place over another type of boundary objects (Boland Jr., & Tenkasi, 1995), called ***prescriptive sketches*** (Ferguson, 1992; Van Der Lugt, 2005).

Developing scientific knowledge, understanding, verstehen, and begreiffen

To theorize is to focus on those entities and relationships in reality that are believed to be central to the observed phenomena – and largely to ignore the rest (Nelson, & Winter, 1982). Such focusing means that we try to grasp tacit knowing, by delimiting the focused experiences from the rest of the tacit knowing, in which they are embedded.

Theory of science often distinguish between three levels of knowledge production and learning: understanding, verstehen, and begreiffen, where understanding corresponds to tacit knowing, verstehen to external knowledge, and begreiffen to scientific knowledge (Philipson, 1980). To ***understand*** our lived lived experience, we need thinking sketches as mediators. To develop a ***verstehen***, we need explicit knowledge informed by others, we need talking sketches as mediators. To achieve a ***begreiffen***, scientific method is required. This scientific knowledge is based on the "common sense", in reality the "coming meaning", achieved by getting a more generalized perspective of our understanding. But based on and ***critically evaluated***, ***4 in figure 24***, as the common meaning can be common prejudice, rather than knowledge. When such scientific knowledge is informing the individual, ***5 in figure 24***, it is understood and embedded in the individual's tacit knowing. When it informs the community of practice it is verstanden, embedded in its negotiated meaning, ***6 in figure 24***.

Figure 24 shows the relationships of the concepts discussed: 1 on pages 169-171; 2 on page174, 3 on pages 175-176. The relationships 4- 6 are only notified here on page 179, but are not further discussed in this book.

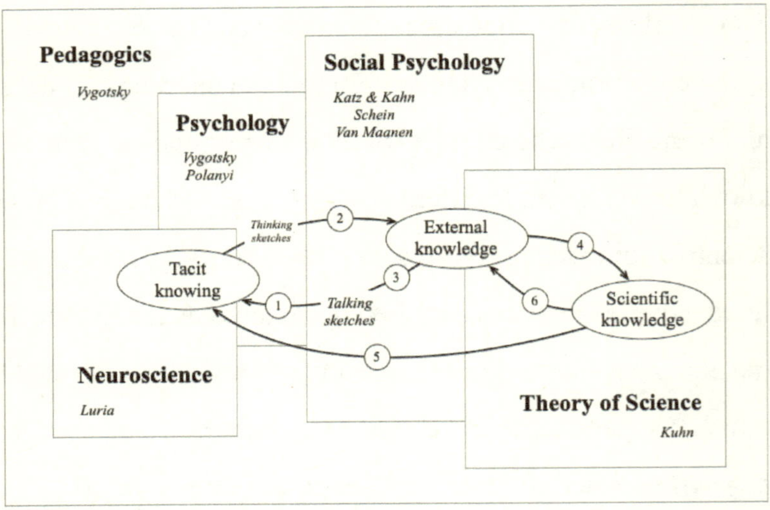

Figure 24. The relations between tacit knowing, externalized knowledge, and scientific knowledge.

12.5 Influence during capitalism requires collaboration!

If the workers are to achieve any influence over the process of production during capitalism, it requires collaboration with the individual capitalist.

In the US, several decades of experiments with union-management cooperation had to contend with significant opposition from leftist factions in the unions; the union leaders involved were accused of class collaboration and lending aid to the enemy while a state of war existed. These socialist trade unionists believed that cooperation was the first step to union control of basic production decisions and government planning. (Jacoby, 1983: 26)

Cooperation between unions and companies is fraught with the same risks that it has raised in the past. On the union side, cooperation leaves the union leadership perpetually open to accusations of collaboration and "sell out". Management is especially concerned that cooperation may infringe on its traditional rights and prerogatives (Jacoby, 1983: 32). Voluntary labor-management cooperation is a fragile phenomenon that flourishes under adverse economic conditions (Jacoby, 1983: 33).

For Jacoby collaboration is a defensive strategy, when the workers have a weak position in the class struggle. Is this necessary? This will be discussed in the case of Korsnäs below.

12.6 Why has capitalism given workers so little influence on the work?[24]

The left has traditionally not seen the impoverishing of the work as a problem.

The dual roles of management can be articulated through a distinction between ***coordinating*** ('directing, superintending and

[24] As seen this section relies on the work of Vidal (2019).

adjusting') the division of labor to increase efficiency and ***disciplining*** labor to ensure the extraction of sufficient output (Vidal, 2019: 176). It is a minority view to see worker participation as a real technical advance in the labor process, which remains limited due to managerial attempts to maintain control (Vidal, 2019: 172).

Braverman and Aglietta saw job enrichment and enlargement programs as superficial forms of employee involvement, driven exclusively by problems with labor control, in particular labor unrest, absenteeism and sabotage under increasing work intensification. In contrast – and consistent with Marx – Gorz and Mallet saw employee-involvement programs as substantive changes in the labor process driven by technical change (Vidal, 2019: 181).

But, because capital relies on the embodied, tacit skills of labor, deskilling was always necessarily incomplete. Even under Taylorism, managers experienced tensions, as they had to harness the tacit skills and cooperation of labor (Vidal, 2019: 188).

Workers' control of production via self-directed teams of polyvalent workers is now at the technological frontier, but the need for capitalists to maintain control means that there will be a continuation of a detailed division of labor and managerial hierarchy (Vidal, 2019: 181-182).

Gordon suggested that managers design the production process to ensure the reproduction of class relations, not by reducing costs, but by adopting practices that are 'better able to discipline the workers, avoid strikes, and extract surplus (Vidal, 2019: 182).

Edwards held that the managerial hierarchy increases profits, by increasing 'control over the labor process, even though 'this profitability does not in general result from greater efficiency. He held that engineers is an ideologically homogenous group, who uniformly enact a clear vision of total capitalist control (Vidal, 2019: 182-183).

Braverman and Noble held that capitalists pursue the absolute deskilling of labor to protect their class-power, while Gordon and Edwards suggested that capitalists prioritize valorization over efficiency (Vidal, 2019: 185).

As the technological frontier shifts from a detailed division of labor, using semiskilled workers, to multi-skilled, substantively empowered workers, there is an emergent threat to capitalist management (Vidal, 2019: 185).

In response to Braverman, Friedman introduced the concept of autonomy ('status, authority and responsibility') and Edwards the concept of bureaucratic control (impersonal regulations set out in company policy, with internal labor markets to induce loyalty). Both suggested that employee-involvement programs are reactive responses to labor–management conflict, or concessions to organized labor, rather than being efficiency-enhancing practices as such (Vidal, 2019: 185).

Following the theoretical development in the 1980s, literature has been dominated by two schools: following Braverman (1974), who see deskilling as the dominant trend, and Friedman and Edwards, who catalogue a range of managerial control regimes. The first school continue to contend that worker participation is a rhetorical device that merely dresses up deskilling and work-intensification (Vidal, 2019: 186).

Mechanical economists, such as Braverman (1974) and Baran, & Sweezy (1970), legitimated a view that the workers will not get a chance to advance their influence under capitalist production and thus that Marx discussion of the forces of production was of little relevance. It has also delayed the questioning of Leninism and other isms, not only as historical examples, but more profoundly as a guideline. But Vidal (2019) is also anchored in mechanical materialism, where class struggle and the aspirations of the working class have no consequence on the evolution of capitalism.

Workers must acquire technical knowledge, organizational capabilities, and systemic understanding of production. Otherwise, democratic governance of production is impossible. "Seizure" leads to substitution, not emancipation.

Worker learning is a necessary condition of transition.

12.7 Capability as the material condition of transition

This chapter has argued that the transformation of capitalism cannot be reduced to changes in ownership or political authority. The decisive issue is the development of workers' capacities to coordinate, plan, and govern production. Such capacities are not given by class position alone, but must be formed through sustained experience, learning, and collective practice within production itself.

Capability sets real limits to this process. While workers may gain influence over parts of the producing and market-relating functions of capital, these gains remain constrained by competitive pressures and the persistence of private ownership.

Yet within these limits, capability formation is possible and historically observable.

Transition must therefore be understood as a process in which workers gradually acquire practical and cognitive mastery over essential functions of production before any comprehensive transformation of ownership can be realized. Without this prior development, attempts to transcend capitalism risk reproducing relations of dependence rather than overcoming them.

As capitalism develops, the direct source of value shifts from isolated labor time toward the social organization of knowledge, science, and cooperation, making workers' collective experience and learning a material condition of production rather than a mere cost factor.

Chapter 12. Learning, Capability, and Temporality: Why Transition Requires Time – Systemic Summery

Workers' collective capabilities can only be developed through practice over time.

Experience accumulates as tacit knowing; tacit knowing is reflected upon collectively and partially externalized as shared understanding.

Only on this basis can formal education transform collective experience into scientific knowledge.

Transition therefore presupposes temporally extended learning processes that cannot be compressed or substituted or decreed by political acts alone.

13. Transition as Suspension, Not Acceleration

The development of capitalism has made the management of production increasingly dependent on scientific knowledge, coordination, and long-term planning. As Marx anticipated, the productive forces now incorporate collective learning and system-wide integration as material elements of production.

Transition beyond capitalism therefore cannot be understood as a single political act or an immediate transformation of ownership. It presupposes that workers acquire influence over increasingly complex productive functions under conditions that allow learning to accumulate and stabilize. Such conditions are historically limited and structurally fragile within capitalism.

Transition must thus be approached as a temporally extended process in which capitalist imperatives are partially suspended or redirected long enough for workers' capacities to develop beyond the limits imposed by price-based competition.

Intensifying price-based competition destroys learning, centralizes power, and produces oligarchy Collapse does not generate capabilities. Acceleration strengthens capitalism's worst tendencies.

13.1 Against Leninist substitution: Why the "socialist" revolutions produced bureaucratic domination

I write this as someone formed by the 1968 generation: by the European student revolt, but also by the most intense class struggles in Western Europe since the 1930s. In Sweden, miners and industrial workers were on strike for months or even half a year. I was organized in – indeed secretary of – a local communist party chapter in the university town of Lund. I had no difficulty distancing myself from Stalin, and I was skeptical toward both Mao and Trotsky. Yet I declared myself Leninist. I read Lenin closely, but not closely enough: I did not examine practice with the same rigor as texts. I began questioning parts of Lenin in my dissertation (Philipson, 1980), yet I held on much longer than I should have. Only when returning to the themes of my thesis did the faultline become unmistakable: on decisive questions Lenin's standpoint departs from Marx and Engels, and in practice often turns antagonistic to their central political premise.

That premise is explicit: workers' emancipation must be the workers' own achievement. It is not a moral slogan; it expresses a material condition. If emancipation is to be real, workers must acquire the knowledge, experience, and organizational capabilities to govern production and society. Where those capacities are absent, "revolution" becomes substitution: one minority replaces another, and hierarchy returns as command.

To call yourself Marxist, when you are trying to do create a society which is the opposite of this vision, you are using new speak to hide the real character of your project. It can be shown that this was the case of all hitherto "socialist" revolutions. Lenin, Trotsky, and Mao (not to mention Stalin) launched authoritarian, undemocratic projects; with no room for the working class, only for their self-elected "representatives", a dictatorship in the name of the proletariat:

> *"With the LT [Lenin-Trotsky] approach, the workers' emancipation through socialist revolution is not so much the result of the "self-activity"* ***(Selbsbetätigung)*** *of the workers themselves (given the appropriate material conditions) as the outcome of the seizure of (state) power by a party (called 'communist') of whole time devoted revolutionaries claiming to be the leaders, the "advanced section"* ***(peredovoi otryad)****, of the working class (supposed to be incapable of developing revolutionary consciousness on its own), acting in its name, and relying on the support of the mass of workers."* (Chattopadhyay, 2003:2; highlighted in the original)

13.2 The Bolshevik coup inside the Soviets

At the end of the First World War, Russian people were exhausted by war, hunger, and the ruling reactionary Tsarist and the liberal cadet party. The February Revolution overthrew the Tsar, and the Provisional Government under the Menshevik Kresinsky emerged – while real power, in practice, was increasingly mediated through the soviets. These councils initially contained a pluralistic political ecology: Socialist Revolutionaries, Mensheviks, the Jewish Bund, Bolsheviks, and independents.

In October 2017 the Bolsheviks made a coup d'état in the democratic soviets and rapidly moved from the slogan "All power to the soviets" to narrowing of representation, the marginalization and later repression of rival socialist currents, and the transformation of plural councils into instruments of one-party rule. The decisive point for this chapter is not simply that a revolution occurred under extreme conditions, but that a specific political solution was chosen and later elevated into doctrine: party substitution for class self-government.

> *"In reality, non-party workers were willing and able to participate in political processes, but, in the Moscow soviet and elsewhere, were pushed out of them by the Bolsheviks. The party's vanguardism, i.e. its conviction that it had the right, and the duty, to make political*

> *decisions on the workers' behalf, was now reinforced by its control of the state apparatus. The working class was politically expropriated; power was progressively concentrated in the party, and specifically in the party elite."* (Pirani, 2008: 4).

Making virtue of the necessity in that labor had not managed to take power in the advanced countries, Lenin declared that Russia was building socialism, without passing through the stage of a democratizing capitalism. He then had to deny the importance of the level of the productive forces as a determining element for the possibility to build socialism, a key element in Marx' theory. At the abortive revolution in 1905, Trotsky still held the traditional Marxist view that one the fundamentally progressive effects of capitalism was the increase of the level of the productive forces. But sometime up to 1917 and the alliance with Lenin, he revised his views.[25] Lenin, Trotsky, and Stalin replaced the dictatorship ***of*** the proletariat by the dictatorship ***in the name of*** the proletariat. In some sense it was a necessity, since there was in Russia a very

---

[25] *"Trotsky later argued that the failure of international revolution to break out was a contingent matter, to be explained in 'subjective' rather than 'objective' terms. It was a consequence of the political failure of revolutionary leaderships, rather than of the supposed 'advantages of backwardness' that quickly became fetters on the Bolsheviks' capacity to move beyond the tasks of developing industry, reforming agriculture, and integrating the 'nation-state', which had been classically associated with bourgeois revolution."* (Smith, 2007: 168)

small proletariat educated by the development of the productive forces. And after the coup d'état in the soviets there were no democratic institution that could be the basis for a democratic capitalism.[26]

The big discussion at the time of the Russian Revolution (or rather at the coup d'état of the Bolsheviks) was whether it was possible to proclaim socialism in one country.; actually, one of the least developed in Europe, with a relatively small working class, with had a limited experience of working with advanced forces of production. Both Rosa Luxemburg and others criticized the Russian revolutionaries for this. But Lenin, Trotsky and others defended themselves for pragmatic reasons: because it was necessary to end the war and because the German working class had failed. Later they made dogma out of necessity. From the beginning, the new government was ***not*** a one-party government. In addition to the Bolsheviks, there were the Mensheviks, the Social Revolutionaries, and the Jewish Arbeiter Bund. But Lenin and Trotsky turned this into a one-party state, even if some of the individuals from other parties remained. Stalin, on the other hand, liquidated almost all of these, the Menshevik Andrey Vyshinsky

---

[26] *"From very early on (1918–19), the Bolsheviks' state was anathema to socialist creativity, emasculating soviets and trades unions, and laying down strict boundaries on workers' political activity, enforced by repressive measures."* (Pirani, 2008: 10).

and Alexandra Kollontai survived. Stalin made Vyshinsky a prosecutor in the Moscow Trials, where the final step was taken by executing almost all the original Central Committee and imposing Stalin's personal dictatorship.

I do not share Trotsky's view, nor the Chinese. We have two questions here, socialism in a country and what is required for it to be socialism. Whether socialism in a country is possible is probably mainly a question of the integrity of the new state, as an island in capitalism. We don't know if such a project is possible or not, but all hitherto such attempts have failed. The problems with socialism are other. The idea that the working class is not capable of leading itself but must have representatives (a Party with capital P, i.e., Leninism). I embraced this idea myself, but realized at the end of the 70s, that it was an error. Not because I shared Rosa Luxemburg's criticism, which became a sweeping criticism against the need for a vanguard (which I still believe is needed, although not necessarily one, but perhaps with advantage several – competition of opinion is good), but above all because it presupposes that under capitalism, a successful struggle for more control by the workers over the means of production is not possible – i.e., they are supposed not to be able to be capable of governing themselves.

13.3 The Russian social-democratic labor party and its factions

Popular resistance against the Tsarist autocratic regime became organized in the Russian social-democratic Labor Party (RSDLP) at its first congress in Minsk 1898 (outside of the Narodnik, later social-revolutionary party, an agrarian populist party, with anarchistic tendencies). The 1998 congress, consisting of several factions, failed to unite on a common program.

The Bund

At the time of the congress the Jewish Arbeiter Bund was the largest socialist group in the empire and was the only party that had worker representation (Tobias, 1965: 394). The chair of the Bund, Arkadi Kremer, was one of the three persons elected to the first central committee of the RSDLP.

As many other Russian and Polish Jewish Marxists – from Leo Trotsky to Rosa Luxemburg – the majority in the Bund did not cultivate any Jewish identity per se but saw themselves as global revolutionaries in the service of humanity (Blomqvist, 2014: 149).

The Bund developed a view of the national dimension and national rights near Austro-Marxism, as formulated by Karl Renner and Otto Bauer (Blomqvist, 2014: 148). As the Austro-

Marxists, the Bund developed its perspective in a multi-ethnic empire but did not conceive the liberation of the Jewish proletariat to be achieved through separation into new nation states. It was ideologically closer to the radical, more cosmopolitan Marxism of Rosa Luxemburg and others, who repudiated all merely national solutions. However, unlike these, who in the name of internationalism rejected the building of a Jewish identity, the Bund was active in asserting, strengthening, and developing such an identity based on socialist ideals (Blomqvist, 2014: 148).

It was not until the second congress, held in Brussels in 1903, that a common program could be taken. Lenin was adamant that the Jewish Bund should not be accepted as a tendency. The relationships between the various Russian Marxist factions were often acrimonious, but those between the Bund and the Bolsheviks were particularly toxic. Lenin led the campaign against the Bund at the Second Congress in 1903, and he and his followers had in the years since then repeatedly denounced the Bund's effort to offer a vision for national revolution (Meyers, 2019: 109). In 1903, the Bund broke with the social democratic Bolshevik majority, when the Bund's position as independent Jewish organization was questioned. At the congress the biggest faction was the Bolsheviks and the smaller the Mensheviks.

On the reunification of Russian Social Democracy in Stockholm 1906, the Bund rejoined.

In the division between the Bolshevists and Mensheviks, the members of the Bund, in general and after some hesitation, came subsequently to belong to the Menshevik side (Blomqvist, 2014: 141).

The Russian workers' movement underwent a series of splits in the years leading up to 1917. The Bund alone entered the Russian Revolution as a unified organization. When the party did split, in 1918-1919 (McGeever, 2017: 252), the result was traumatic (Meyers, 2019: 109)

The Bolsheviks tried to picture both the Bund and the social revolutionaries as non-workers parties. Lenin depicted the Bund as a movement composed mainly, if not only of Jewish artisans; of those semi-proletarian elements who stand with one foot in the camp of the working class and with the other in the camp of the petty bourgeoisie (Tobias, 1965: 402). While this was true to some extent, it was the character of a large part of the Russian working class, which due to the backwardness of the Russian empire was newly constituted as a class, often going back and forth between industrial and rural subsistence.[27]

Even though revolutionary politics were incompatible with antisemitism for the Bolshevik leadership, yet when it came to the party rank and file, the overlap between revolutionary Bolshevism and antisemitism was real in 1917 (McGeever, 2017: 245). When hundreds of thousands of workers protested in Petrograd on 18 June, Bolsheviks tore down Bundist banners and shouted antisemitic slogans (McGeever, 2017: 246). Events in 1918 and 1919 would reveal just how acute this problem was, when in many regions the Red Army found swathes of pogromists in their midst, marching behind the slogan "Smash the Yids, long live Soviet Power!" (McGeever, 2017: 248).

Ukraine was the setting for unimaginable butchery in 1919 and was also home to approximately half of the Bund's total membership during the Russian Revolution (Meyers, 2019: 108) In the spring of 1918, Bolshevik power was consolidated through anti-Jewish violence by the local cadres of the party and Red

---

[27] This was to an even higher extent the case with the social revolutionaries, but in many cases they ended up as legitimate representatives of the workers against the Bolsheviks; as in February 1921, when the metalworkers, traditionally a strong base of the Bolsheviks, rounded in angrily on the party and not only denounced the rationing policy, but also adopted a resolution moved by SR sympathizers (Pirani, 2004: 147).

Guards in northeast Ukraine (McGeever, 2017:250-251). This also had consequences for modern history, as drawing on the political support that the Zionists received from the British Empire and the success of the British military in the Middle East, they surged ahead of the Bund as representative of Jewish workers (Meyers, 2019: 114).

The Social Revolutionaries

The social revolutionaries was a socialist party with an anarchist trait, with a predecessor in the Narodnik. It was a party of serf-like, rather than independent peasants. Their strive was for freedom from the bonds to the noble owners, but also to get land to cultivate themselves. Even if they were serfs, their strive was petty-bourgeoise.

The Mensheviks

The Mensheviks have been considered as less “radical” than the Bolsheviks, because they opposed the Bolshevik coup d’état in the soviets, but the Mensheviks regarded itself as orthodox Marxist revolutionaries, in contrast to what they saw as the utopian, voluntarian and terroristic Bolshevism. Socialism was, as they saw it, an unavoidable historical consequence of capitalism’s development, but which could only come about, as Marx explained, ***when capitalism’s productive forces broke the old***

shackles. holding back the forces of production (Blomqvist, 2014: 147). [My emphasizes]. They believed that ***Bolshevism turned Marx upside down*** (Blomqvist, 2014: 147). [My emphasizes]

The Bolsheviks

What was the character of this party representing what Lenin and Trotsky considered to be the most "advanced section" of the proletariat?[28]

The Bolsheviks were an exile party – except Prehobatiensky's small "Group for the Emancipation of Labor" in Russia, consisting of middle-class intellectuals. An exception was the Parisian community of Bolsheviks, including Bogdanov's group of workers in Paris (Allen, 2005: 3). Through its member Shlapinikov, this group inspired the later independent workers' opposition. It seems unlikely that the Bolsheviks ever was a working-class party (Allen, 2005: 3). In mid-late 1917, Lenin's pre-revolutionary conception of a small conspiratorial party was discarded as the doors were opened wide to tens of thousands of

[28] The Chinese communist party was from the beginning a peasant party. Mao Tse-Tung was a peasant leader, with no experience in the struggle of the labor class or unionism. Mao Tsetung co-opted Chou-En-Lai to get legitimacy, but the latter had already lost his base after Chang-Kai check destroyed the Shanghai workers' movement in 1927. Later the CCP class character was state officers, military and "red" directors.

new members, many of whom were politicized for the first time (McGeever, 2017: 248).

The uprising in Kronstadt against the Bolsheviks, did not get any active support in Moscow. During the Kronstadt events sympathy translate into action only a few occasions. Workers at the Bromlei factory, who passed a resolution supporting Kronstadt, were punished with arrests, and mass sacking of the entire workforce and selective re-employment, which in turn triggered some solidarity strikes in nearby factories. (Pirani, 2004: 149)

The 1921 workers' movement was the effect of workers having become, "de-proletarianized" according to Lenin. But the evidence from Moscow shows that the metalworkers, who were less seriously affected than others by the dispersals and disruptions of the war and civil war, were central to the movement. Activists with long records in the workers' movement participated in it. Available evidence also throws doubt on Soviet-era assumptions that the movement was led by the opposition socialist parties, an argument often made by Soviet historians, and by some of their Western counterparts, who relied largely on Menshevik and SR sources. (Pirani, 2004: 156-157)

During the opposition movements among workers in 1921-1923, it was with the help of office workers and the army that Bolsheviks gained a majority to strike it down. 42% of the metal workers', 71% of the leather workers' and 66% of the food workers' delegates were non-party. Only textile workers and the military garrison produced Bolshevik majorities. The chemical workers, who had previously supported the Mensheviks, voted 50% Bolshevik (Pirani, 2004: 151). The Bolsheviks lost support more heavily in the larger enterprises (Pirani, 2004: 150). The state and Party were relying on "specialists" of suspect social origins to run industry and staff governmental bodies (Allen, 2005: 7).

The mobilization of the most dedicated revolutionaries to fight the civil war had depopulated the Party, as well as the trade unions, of their most "conscious" members, who had either fallen on the front or. become military officers. Shliapnikov warned that "hostile" elements had infiltrated the Party's ranks in their stead (Allen, 2005:9).

13.4 The Soviets

The soviets were a popular movement to overthrow the Tsarist rule. The Russian parliament, the Duma, did not have a popular legitimacy, as it was not democratically elected.

Between March and November 1917, soviet elections moved from their initial form (direct, unmediated elections from bodies of workers, soldiers, peasants, etc.), to competing party lists (Pirani, 2004: 143). Many workers, who earlier in the year had expressed non-partyism in various ways, moved in October-November to support the Bolshevik stance on soviet power (Pirani, 2004: 144).

Lenin was from the very beginning negative to the soviets but used them to make a coup d'état to get the Bolsheviks absolute power. Publicly he demanded 'all power to the soviets', but in private communication with party leaders, he showed utter distrust, if not disdain, for the soviet power. He attempted to persuade the leadership that the party must seize power 'alone', ignoring the soviets. (Chattopadhyay, 2003:2)

Workers' councils have been a key element in many 20th century visions of democratic socialism, whether in the construction of the Soviet Union or in Gramsci's Prison Notebooks (Gramsci, 1971). But they have only existed for a short while.

13.5 The dictatorship of the Bolsheviks

The workers did not trust the Mensheviks and the Social Revolutionaries, but stopped voting for the Bolsheviks (Pirani,

2004: 151). Where it was most organized, the non-party tendency appears to have been a loose coalition of the egalitarian workers, who had supported the Bolsheviks in October, but had become disillusioned, and Social Revolutionaries (particularly left) and Mensheviks. They valued their links with other workers more highly, than their participation in party groupings. They were the Cheka's chief targets (Pirani, 2004: 153).

The repression of Mensheviks, Social Revolutionaries, and anarchists was one factor in the growth of the non-party bloc, but not the only one. The non-party tendency reflected a strong desire for more democratic types of soviet rule. On issues of democracy, the egalitarian workers were allied with the Social Revolutionaries and Mensheviks against the Bolsheviks (Pirani, 2004: 148). Where the non-party bloc was more organized, it embraced both workers with Menshevik and Social Revolutionary sympathies and those who had supported the Bolsheviks in 1917. The question that deeply divided this tendency from the Bolsheviks, was participatory democracy, to which the Bolsheviks were in practice opposed (Pirani, 2004: 157).

Lists of non-party candidates were organized in most of the big factories and often defeated Bolshevik lists (Pirani, 2004: 150). Those who voted for non-party candidates were first and foremost striving towards some sort of soviet rule, with broader participation and without the Bolsheviks' dictatorial impositions (Pirani, 2004: 151). When the newly elected soviet convened for the first time on 13 May 1921, a group of non-partyists tried to turn the disillusionment with Bolshevism expressed at the polls into a constructive opposition in the soviet's executive bodies – and were blocked by the Bolshevik majority based on ***sluzhashchie*** [bureaucrats and office workers] (Pirani, 2004: 152). For the mainstream Bolshevik majority, such democracy was positively dangerous. Instead, they sought to bring non-party workers into the apparatus ***to counter the predominance of the middle class*** [My emphasizes], and approved of non-party workers taking responsibility for production, welfare, and other carefully defined tasks in factories – but allowed non-party workers into decision-making bodies only 'under party leadership (Pirani, 2004: 155-156). The workers that were recruited were workers with a very high potential for upward mobility (Unger, 1977: 313).

In 1921-22, after the end of the Civil War, the leading Mensheviks were forced to choose between banishment to Siberia or going into exile (Blomqvist, 2014: 145). Kamenev made clear that the Bolsheviks would no more accept non-partyism as a soviet tendency, than they would accept Mensheviks, Social

Revolutionaries, or anarchists (Pirani, 2004: 153). The Bolsheviks made no effort to collaborate with the non-partyists and hastened the eradication of soviet democracy and the triumph of the anti-democratic one-party state (Pirani, 2004: 157). In March 1921, the Workers' Opposition was banned (Allen, 2005: 16).

The Politburo, composed of Bukharin, Lenin, and Krestinsky, decided that for Party members at nonparty congresses to pass resolutions contradicting resolutions of the CC would be

> *"...incorrect and inadmissible from the point of view of Party discipline."* (Allen, 2005: 14).

The left opposition within the Bolsheviks become a unified group with its own platform only at the Eight Congress of Soviets in late December 1920, when Kollontai recalled the Party had already split into three groups, centered on Lenin, Trotsky, and Bukharin. Kollontai argued that the Workers' Opposition members formed a faction only after Party leaders had done the same, and she emphasized its popular roots (Allen, 2005: 16).

Confronted with worker defiance, Lenin reacted exactly as had Nicholas II, he turned to the military. But whereas the last tsar soon caved in, Lenin was prepared to go to any length to stay in power. In February 1917, the main source of disaffection had been the garrison, now it was the factory (Pirani, 2004: 160).[29]

13.6 Productive forces, temporality, and "making a virtue of necessity"

Marx's position is structurally clear: socialism presupposes a level of productive forces and worker capabilities such that workers can collectively govern production. Lenin faced an objective dilemma: Russia was economically backward, with a relatively small and unevenly developed proletariat, and the hoped-for revolutions in advanced capitalist countries failed. Under these conditions, Bolshevik leaders made a strategic and political move: they treated necessity as virtue and declared that "socialism" could be built without passing through a long phase of democratizing capitalist development.

---

[29] To control the soviets, Lenin infused them with the Bolshevik ***party***, and to take control of the party Stalin infused the party with state functionaries. Stalin was uninterested in whether the party had a worker representation or not, for him it was important that it represented ***the state apparatus***. After Stalin's death the new leadership wanted to increase workers' representation, but it seems to have been only to get more legitimacy, since the installed a quota of workers in the party, but wanted to preserve the state representation, so the quota was a function of the number of state officers they wanted to include. It also seems that many of those listed as workers was quickly given posts in the administration (Rigby, 1976: 332). The party was still a male party, where the women were only 20-25% of the membership (Rigby, 1976: 224). Thus, with Stalin, the monopoly of the party becomes the monopoly of the state.

But this required a theoretical displacement. The development of workers' capacities – central in Marx and Engels – was no longer treated as a prerequisite for emancipation. It became something the party would deliver to the workers through command, planning, and discipline. The dictatorship of the proletariat was replaced by dictatorship in the name of the proletariat.

This is the mechanism of substitution: when capability is absent, command fills the gap. But command does not generate capability; it generates obedience, hierarchy, and dependence. It can mobilize, coerce, and reorganize. It cannot substitute for the slow, collective, experiential learning through which workers become capable of governing.

13.7 Soviets, unions, and the suppression of worker self-government

The great internal conflict after 1917 was not merely "plan versus market" or "centralization versus decentralization", but whether workers' councils and unions would be institutions of worker rule – or subordinate transmission belts of the party-state.

Where workers attempted to defend participatory soviet democracy and union influence over production, the party increasingly treated such democracy as dangerous and blocked it through party discipline, coercion, and reliance on non-proletarian administrative strata (bureaucracy, office workers, coercive apparatus).

13.8 Taylorism, Fordism, and the mis-recognition of "Modernity"

Leninist practice repeatedly equated "modernity" with the most coercive methods of capitalist labor control. Taylorism and Fordism were treated as neutral techniques: instruments to raise productivity, to be adopted regardless of their class content. But these methods were historically designed to separate conception from execution, to centralize knowledge in management, and to reduce workers' autonomy in the labor process.

Here the contradiction becomes explicit: a politics that claims emancipation installs labor-process forms that block the development of worker capabilities and control. The result is predictable. When workers are ordered to obey "one-man management," when specialists govern while workers remain subordinate, the system reproduces the separation between those who command and those who execute. The form may be "red," but the social relation remains hierarchical.

13.9 The Bund and the problem of democratic pluralism

A politics that cannot tolerate pluralism in the workers' movement cannot produce democratic self-government after revolution.

13.10 "Red" directors

Lenin and Trotsky installed "red directors" to manage the enterprises and used them to suppress the influence of trade unions, soviets, and even the local party cells. Lenin was pressing a plan for one-man management of industry, which would replace the collegial system, in which trade union representatives participated (Allen, 2005: 13). According to Lenin, the masses must, show the "…unquestioning obedience to the single will of the leaders of the labor process…" and must accept unquestioning subordination during working time to the one-person decision of the soviet directors, elected or nominated by soviet institutions and provided with dictatorial powers (Chattopadhyay, 2003: 4).

The left-communist Shliapnikov's attacked the practice of relying on technical and managerial specialists to run industry, rather than training workers to do so. Shliapnikov was certain that Trotsky's plan for "militarization of the working class" would destroy worker initiative. Most union leaders were aligned against Trotsky and many of them were alarmed by Lenin's plan for one-man management. (Allen, 2005: 8-13)

Fascists, the revolutionary right, socialists, and communists all hailed the most oppressive methods of capitalism, Taylorism and Fordism, as advanced and progressive. Lenin, Trotsky, and Gramsci all saw it necessary to employ the most 'modern' methods of capitalism, whether these were oppressive or not; whether these methods deprived the workers any influence over the work process or not; whether it deskilled them, or not. The anti-Taylor faction was a product of an inner Communist Party controversy between Lenin and the Left Communists. Those to the left of Lenin felt that capitalist means, such as scientific management, could not be used to achieve socialist ends, but must be fundamentally altered to serve the worker's interests. (Wren, & Bedeian, 2004: 291) Pavel Kerzhentsev, a Left Communist, argued that Taylorism was unscientific and would never fulfill the objectives of scientific Marxism (Wren, & Bedeian, 2004: 291).

Lenin and Trotsky tried to spread Taylorism in the Soviet Union. However, with limited success, not because it was just a 'progressive' rhetoric (as stated by Wren, & Bedeian, 2004), but because it became subordinate to the day-to-day politics of the struggling Bolshevik party. The party suppressed the trade unions and installed managers that run the factories in the name of the party. No room for workers' influence here. The workers got the protestant ethic pushed on them by communist leaders, who most of them had limited or no experience as industrial workers. The workers were not considered mature enough to evolve their own morals. The Bolsheviks succeeded to improve the economy by Stayanowish workers, with longer working hours, increased intensity of the work, and earlier death. (Wren, & Bedeian, 2004)

Trotsky, who in his youth (1904) had, in the name of the "self-activity of the proletariat," denounced Lenin's 'political substitutionism' of the party for the proletariat, completely reversed his position after his conversion to Leninism circa 1917. (Chattopadhyay, 2003: 2).

Gramsci's utopia, developed in his essay 'Americanism and Fordism', was unequivocally Fordist. Gramsci saw Fordism as deriving 'from an inherent necessity to achieve the organization of a planned economy. Thus, Fordism represents the 'ultimate stage' (Gramsci, 1971: 280) of the socialization of the forces of production, based on the subordination under financial to industrial capital and the creation of a new form of morality. Lenin, Trotsky and Gramsci meant that it was necessary to 'discipline' the workers by these methods. Gramsci agrees with Trotsky that the crisis can only be resolved by the exercise of coercion by an elite of the class, but he argues that Trotsky erred in proposing a purely repressive solution, through the militarization of labor, rather than recognizing the need for the development of self-discipline. For Henry Ford, the anti-Semite and active Nazi, the essence was to install discipline and Protestant moral in the workers (Clarke, 1990: 136-138).

Lenin's economic advisers, Milyutin and Larin, drew explicitly on the notions of the right-wing CEO of AEG, Rathenau and his engineer Moellendorff (Maier, 1970: 50-51).

That this subordination of the workers to capitalist methods was not just a short-term adaption to national defense was shown by that they did nothing to prepare for a future of another kind. Shliapnikov criticized the Commissariat of Enlightenment for having done little to establish evening schools for workers (Allen, 2005: 8); thus, to prepare them for a future more important role in the management of industry.

13.11 Plan, market, and the contemporary form of "coordination"

The old opposition "plan versus market" has become analytically misleading. When the so-called Soviet Union introduced planning, capitalism was still underdeveloped and the contrast between plan and market seemed enormous. Contemporary capitalism coordinates vast distributed production through supply chains and ecosystems that involve planning inside and across firms, combined with competitive rivalry between ecosystems. Capitalism has acquired a high degree of conditional planning – without becoming socialist.

The competition between ecosystems, are not the planning of a central planning authority, but I don't see in what such a bureaucracy would be more socialist than ecosystems run by workers' councils, even if they are competing. And such a competition must not be based on value-production in the capitalist surplus-value sense, but value evaluated by panels of users or some other means, which we don't know yet. Many of the instruments of capitalist market research can be used (and developed) to construct use-value measures. The goal of such an ecosystem would then be to maximize use-value to minimal cost (including e.g. environmental costs). For why should the end-customer have no choices during socialism?

The relevant question is therefore not whether coordination exists (it always does), but who controls it and to what end. A socialist transition worth the name would mean coordination governed by workers and users, oriented toward use-value (including environmental and social costs), not toward surplus-value. Competition, if it persists, must be competition in use-value and innovation under democratic constraints, not price-based competition that destroys learning and concentrates power. This returns us to the central theme: a democratic transition requires institutions that protect capability formation, stabilize value-based regimes, and prevent the reassertion of destructive price discipline.

13.12 Why did the Russian revolution not deliver freedom?

The most effective defense of the revolution is one in which the workers and peasants have a direct influence – a "material stake" in the making of decisions (as well as receiving socioeconomic benefits). Bureaucratic centralism and political commandism do not raise consciousness through practice, but through exhortation in a plebiscatory fashion. Popularly elected organs that discuss and debate issues and elect their leaders create greater identity with policies and leaders and are more capable of eliciting the sacrifices necessary to carry on sustained warfare, even at high material cost. (Petras, 1983: 117)

The revolution is not a reified "thing" to be defended. It is meaningful only when it embodies the great majority of the working masses in a supreme effort to change their lives. That is why revolutionary wars are so successful against innumerable enemies and great material odds (from the Soviet Union of 1917 to Vietnam in 1975) and why they fail and are defeated when they try to pigeon-hole "national defense" in one phase and social transformation in another; as in Spain in 1936-1939 (Petras, 1983: 118).

The problem of security and national defense should never impinge on the ***principle*** of the autonomy of the working class, the right of the laboring classes to elect their revolutionary leaders, the right to criticize, etc., whatever the nature of the crises, ***even when it is necessary to temporarily suspend the exercise of those right in the face of imminent invasion's*** (Petras, 1983: 118).

Just as democratic control heightens workers' and peasants' capacity for military struggle, so does democratic control over production heighten their willingness to produce and sacrifice for the ***future*** (Petras, 1983: 119).

“The Progressives always held an ambivalent attitude toward participatory democracy, although they welcomed expanded participation if accompanied by responsible leadership." (Jacoby, 1983: 20)

Modern "leftists", e.g. Peña (2014: 267), promote the Leninist ideology that is substituting Marx dictatorship of the proletariat with the dictatorship of a communist party. But these so-called leftists are in fact nationalists:

> *"Cultivation of the proper* ***national cultural characteristics*** *is vital to the creation of a sustainable society, for a socialist culture is necessary for promoting the social management of sustainable development."* (Peña, 2014: 272; Italics in the original).

13.13 The core proposition: No emancipation without capability

The argument of this book implies a strict criterion for distinguishing emancipation from substitution:

- Political control cannot substitute for knowledge, experience, and coordination.
- Transition without capability produces bureaucratic domination.

This is exactly what the temporality argument implies: where capability formation has not occurred, command substitutes – and emancipation becomes impossible.

This is why Leninism is not merely a moral failure or a contingent historical deviation. It is a structural political response to a structural problem: attempting to overcome capitalism where the material prerequisites for worker self-government have not been developed – and then treating party command as a substitute for that development. Leninism was confusing systemic tendency with historical necessity, confusing centralization with capacity, and confusing political substitution with self-emancipation.

Thus, political control cannot substitute for experience, knowledge, and coordination. Command reproduces hierarchy, when learning is absent.

Conclusion

Transition without capability leads to bureaucratic domination.

Chapter 13.
Transition as Suspension, Not Acceleration – Systemic Summery

Where collective capability formation has not occurred, command necessarily substitutes for self-rule.

Without workers capable of managing the producing and market-relating functions of capital, changes in ownership reproduce the subsumption of the collective worker rather than abolish it.

Historically, twentieth century 'socialist' revolutions legitimated this substitution through Newspeak (Orwell): proclaiming workers' power ,while instituting rule over workers.

14. From Concentration to Oligarchy: Political Consequences

Over recent decades, advanced capitalist economies have experienced a marked concentration of economic power, accompanied by rising inequality and growing strain on democratic institutions. These developments are no longer contested; what remains are to grasp their origins and their implications for political order.

Capitalist competition has never been uniform. Historically, different forms of competition have produced different developmental trajectories, different firm structures, and different political consequences. What matters here is not the theoretical distinction itself, but its cumulative political effects.

14.1 Divergent market outcomes under price-based competition

Over time, competitive pressures in capitalism tend to favor scale, cost compression, and organizational simplification. In some sectors this leads to industrial collapse; in others it produces monopolies or oligopolies. In both cases, competitive pluralism erodes. What appears as competitive pressure at the firm level accumulates, over time, into systemic political effects.

Railways, characterized by high fixed costs and infrastructural indispensability, historically experienced underinvestment under price pressure, declining reliability, and eventual collapse or re-nationalization.

Digital Platforms, by contrast, are structured around network effects, data accumulation, and winner-take-all dynamics, leading to rapid concentration and infrastructural dominance.

These markets illustrate how structural conditions determine whether price strategy destroys competition (value markets) or distorts it by accelerating concentration (scale markets).

Supply-chain fragility as a secondary effect

As concentration advances, its effects cascade through supply chains, hollowing out capabilities, increasing fragility, and transferring risk downward. What appears as efficiency at the centre often produces systemic vulnerability at the periphery.

Procurement systems reinforce this dynamic when they prioritize lowest price, rather than capability development, reliability, or long-term fit. Capability-based procurement becomes a critical condition in value-driven industries.

14.2 Institutional drift in competition policy

The structural effects of misapplied price logic do not unfold in a vacuum. They interact with and are amplified by the institutional frameworks that govern competition. In recent decades, competition policy in many economies has undergone a profound shift: from structural concerns about concentration and dominance, to narrow evaluations of short-term price effects. This shift – commonly described as institutional drift – has played a central role in enabling market concentration.

From structural antitrust to price effects

Traditional antitrust policy emphasized market structure, barriers to entry, and the long-term distribution of economic power. Enforcement was oriented towards preserving pluralism and preventing dominance.

From the late twentieth century onward, competition policy was reshaped by a neoclassical interpretation of markets. Regulators increasingly accepted arguments that concentration is efficient, dominance is not problematic, unless prices rise. They hold that market forces will correct distortions, and structural interventions (e.g., breakups) are unnecessary.

This transformation effectively aligned competition policy with price-based competition, treating price levels rather than structural dynamics as the decisive criterion.

Why drift occurred

Understanding institutional drift as a mere policy failure or ideological shift is analytically insufficient (Hacker & Pierson, 2010; Streeck, 2011). Institutional drift did not occur in isolation. It evolved alongside changes in industrial structure, professional expertise, and political coalitions.

Thus, drift emerges through changing industrial structures, lobbying by firms benefiting from scale, epistemic capture of regulators, professional networks linking economists, lawyers, and policy analysts. These slow, subtle processes reshape public institutions without overt political conflict.

Regulatory feedback and reinforcement

Institutional drift does not merely weaken enforcement – it creates a feedback loop that stabilizes and expands concentration. Once competition policy defines harm exclusively in price terms, value-driven industries receive no protection, capability destruction goes unrecognized, tipping dynamics are ignored, dominant firms acquire political influence, and regulators become dependent on industry expertise.

This feedback loop makes concentrated markets appear “normal”, and because regulators no longer see structural power as a problem, the conditions for pluralistic competition erode further.

Drift as an organizational phenomenon

From the perspective of organization theory, institutional drift is not merely a shift in legal doctrine – it is a transformation in how state agencies interpret their environment, evaluate evidence, and understand their own mission. These interpretive frames evolve through professionalization, and networks of expertise across institutional fields.

Thus, competition authorities increasingly adopt firm-centered analytical tools, efficiency metrics, narrow welfare indicators, deference to industry claims. Thus, weakening the structural oversight role they once played.

As institutional drift normalizes concentration and weakens regulatory constraints, dominant firms accumulate new forms of power – both structural and infrastructural – that extend beyond market outcomes (Lindblom, 1977; Winters, 2011).

14.3 The rise of oligarchic capitalism

As competition policy drifts towards price-only criteria and markets are restructured, dominant firms accumulate power that extend far beyond commercial advantage. These firms can shape market rules, influence state action, and structuring social and economic life. This transformation corresponds to what Lindblom (1977) and Winters (2011) describe as oligarchic capitalism.

Oligarchic capitalism is characterized by the concentration of economic and institutional capacities in a small number of firms, whose decisions have system-wide consequences. In this context, market concentration is not merely an economic outcome; it is a political and organizational phenomenon (Winters, 2011).

Structural power: The capacity to constrain the state

Structural power arises when firms become so central to the functioning of an economy that governments cannot easily regulate or discipline them, without risking negative macroeconomic effects (Lindblom, 1977).

Infrastructural power: Private actors governing public systems

Infrastructural power refers to the capacity of organizations to structure the environments within which others act. Digital platforms, logistics networks, and financial infrastructures increasingly govern communication, visibility, information flows, and market access. When firms provide infrastructural services that become essential to economic and social participation, the decisions – pricing, ranking, access, interoperability – acquire quasi-regulatory authority. This represents a profound shift: Market dominance becomes a mode of governance.

Discursive power: Shaping what appears thinkable

Large firms increasingly influence public narratives, policy frames, regulatory discourse, academic expertise, and managerial ideology. They do so by funding research, shaping media narratives, participating in policy design, and providing the technical language through which markets are understood.

Discursive power reinforces structural and infrastructural power, by shaping what regulators, managers, and the public perceive as legitimate, efficient, or inevitable (Hirschman & Berman, 2014).

The consolidation of oligarchic power does not require coordination or conspiracy. It emerges from structural dependencies created by concentration itself.

Together, these forms of power translate economic concentration into durable political asymmetry.

14.4 Why this matters for democracy

Democracy requires the dispersion of economic power (Streeck, 2011).

When a small number of firms control the infrastructure of public life, the conditions for political equality erode.

Representative institutions depend on countervailing power. Oligarchic capitalism produces the opposite: a configuration where firms become co-legislators of market structure, co-administrators of public services, and arbiters of economic opportunity (Lindblom, 1977; Streeck, 2011).

This is not simply an economic problem – it is a constitutional one (Winters, 2011).

Price-based competition tends toward concentration. Concentration produces structural power. Structural power corrodes democratic institutions.

Democracy depends on the dispersion of economic and institutional power. In pluralistic economies with many firms, no single actor can dominate markets, shape state agendas, or control the infrastructures through which citizens communicate and participate. As concentration increases, these conditions shift. Dominant firms accumulate structural, infrastructural, and discursive power, undermining the foundations on which democratic governance rests (Lindblom, 1977; Winters, 2011; Zuboff, 2019).

14.5 Structural power and the erosion of public autonomy

Structural power allows dominant firms to influence public policy simply by virtue of their centrality within the economy. Governments become reluctant to impose regulations that might reduce investment, employment, or short-term economic stability.

Structural power operates through investment threats, regulatory chill, and growing state dependency on private infrastructures.

Over time, the state's capacity to act independently diminishes, not because of formal capture, but because policy choices are constrained by economic dependencies that concentrated markets themselves have produced (Lindblom, 1977).

14.6 Infrastructural power and the privatization of public space

Digital and logistical infrastructures increasingly mediate communication, commerce, mobility, information flows, and political participation.

Firms controlling these infrastructures can determine who is visible or invisible; set rules for participation, structure access to markets, influence public discourse, and enforce private governance systems.

Infrastructural dominance effectively relocates core democratic functions – such as public deliberation, agenda-setting, and even access to economic participation – into privately governed systems with limited accountability (Pistor, 2019).

14.7 Discursive power and the narrowing of democratic imagination

Dominant actors shape problem definitions, policy narratives, and regulatory assumptions.

Large firms influence discourse by funding think tanks, supporting academic research, dominating media ecosystems, shaping policy narratives.

As discursive frames narrow, democratic societies lose the capacity to imagine alternatives to concentrated markets or to recognize the structural origins of economic power.

14.8 Oligarchic drift: When economic inequality becomes political inequality

Oligarchy emerges when wealth and economic power translate into political influence. Concentration intensifies this process by giving dominant firms the resources to influence elections, privileged access to policymakers, control over communication channels, and the ability to set regulatory agendas.

The drift towards oligarchic capitalism is therefore not simply an economic trend, but a political transformation: economic inequality becomes political inequality, as dominant firms accumulate capacities once reserved for public institutions.

14.9 Democratic fragility

As pluralism erodes, the institutional foundations necessary for democratic resilience – independent firms, diverse economic bases, countervailing power – are weakened. Democracy becomes increasingly vulnerable to structural economic domination.

Given these structural and political consequences, chapter 14 identifies the conceptual, institutional, and organizational reforms needed to restore competitive pluralism and strengthen democratic institutions.

Chapter 14.
From concentration to Oligarchy: Political Consequences – Systemic Summery

Left to its inherent tendencies, capitalism tends toward concentration and oligarchy: the rule of a small number of capitals, whose structural power subordinates both state and society.

Under oligarchic conditions, pluralism erodes, bourgeois democracy weakens, and the institutional and organizational space required for collective capability contracts or becomes structurally unstable.

Class struggle therefore cannot be confined to distribution. It must also resist concentration and build institutions capable of defending bourgeois democracy and stabilizing value-based competition.

15. What Must Change: Conceptual, Institutional, Organizational, and Democratic Reforms

The undermining of democracy requires reforms at multiple levels – conceptual, organizational, institutional, and democratic. These reforms are not independent; each targets a different stage of protecting the development of workers' capabilities development and institutional structures to protect these.

15.1 Institutional reform: Restoring structural antitrust and countervailing power

Because misalignment interacts with institutional drift, conceptual reform must be paired with changes in the regulatory frameworks governing competition (Khan, 2019).

Competition policy should (Sutton, 1991, 1998):

- focus on market structure, not short-term price effects
- identify and intervene in tipping dynamics
- address dominance in infrastructural markets
- rebuild institutional capacity to evaluate structural harms

Reviving structural antitrust would re-establish the conditions for pluralistic competition, reduce the systemic dependencies that fuel structural power, and counteract the political effects of oligarchic concentration.

Institutional reform also requires rebuilding countervailing power – labor organizations, professional associations, public agencies, and local institutions capable of constraining dominant firms and sustaining competitive pluralism (Polanyi, 1944; Khan, 2019).

15.2 Organizational reform: Reorienting firms toward capability-based competition

Reforms must also target firms themselves. Organizations embedded in value-driven markets require strategies that priorities workforce development, supplier capability building, innovation, long-term investment, and system reliability (Penrose, 1959; Teece, Pisano, & Shuen, 1997; Chandler, 1962; Philipson, 2020b, 2022a).

Price-based competition erodes these foundations.

Capability-based procurement should be adopted to prevent supply-chain degradation and ensure that focal firms do not impose cost structures that hollow out the very ecosystems they depend on. Procurement systems must incorporate criteria such as reliability, learning potential, and long-term fit, not merely lowest price.

Organizations should also implement internal governance structures – metrics, incentives, reporting systems – that privilege long-term capability formation over short-term cost reductions. In capability-intensive industries, such changes are prerequisites for competitive sustainability (Polanyi, 1944; March, 1991).

15.3 Democratic reform: Rebuilding the institutional architecture of pluralism

Democracy depends on the dispersion of economic power. When competitive pluralism erodes, democratic institutions weaken.

Democratic governance requires:

- effective state oversight of infrastructural markets
- institutions capable of counterbalancing dominant firms
- transparency around platform governance
- protections for economic autonomy and voice

These reforms are not external to organizational life, but direct responses to the organizational mechanisms described earlier. Concentration becomes politically dangerous when firms acquire infrastructural and structural power; limiting these powers is therefore a democratic imperative.

A democratic political economy must ensure that no firm becomes indispensable to public communication, commerce, or political coordination. Rebuilding institutional checks on private infrastructural power is central to the future viability of democratic governance.

15.4 Integrating reforms across the tendencies of capitalism

Organizational reform targets firm strategy: institutional reform targets the regulatory feedback loop; and democratic reform targets the political consequences of concentration. Together, these interventions address the multilevel dynamics through which price-based competition contributes to democratic fragility.

The final section synthesizes the argument and highlights its implications for organization theory, political economy, and future research.

15.5 What a democratic political economy requires

A democratic political economy cannot be secured by markets alone. It depends on the sustained plurality of capitals, on institutional limits to concentration, and on the active development of workers' productive capabilities through class struggle. Where these conditions erode, democracy becomes fragile regardless of formal political rights.

At a minimum, five conditions must be protected:

First, value-based competition must be preserved. Only where competition operates through quality, learning, and differentiation does capitalism create space for the development of workers' knowledge, discretion, and collective capabilities. Price-based competition, when generalized, undermines these capacities and accelerates concentration.

Second, structural antitrust is essential. Competition policy must act on market structure, not merely outcomes. Without limits on scale, dominance, and tipping dynamics, economic power accumulates to levels that overwhelm both firms and states. Structural antitrust is therefore not an efficiency instrument, but a democratic one.

Third, capability-based procurement and governance must replace lowest-price logic in value-sensitive sectors. Firms and public agencies that rely on price-only criteria systematically degrade their own productive ecosystems. Long-term reliability, learning potential, and cooperative capacity are preconditions for sustainable competition and democratic resilience.

Fourth, work organization must be learning-centered. The development of workers' capabilities – technical, organizational, and social – is not a by-product of capitalism, but the outcome of struggle over how production is organized. Without institutionalized access to learning, participation, and influence, workers' liberation cannot occur, and democratic promises collapse into new forms of domination.

Finally, institutions must lengthen temporality. Democracy requires time horizons that exceed quarterly returns and electoral cycles. Institutions that stabilize investment, protect learning processes, and buffer productive systems from short-term shocks are necessary to prevent capitalism's crisis tendencies from translating into authoritarian outcomes.

Democracy thus depends not on markets as such, but on the plurality of capitals and on continuous class struggle to limit the brutalizing tendencies of capitalism while expanding its democratizing ones.

A democratic political economy requires the protection of value-based competition against premature price discipline; institutional arrangements capable of limiting concentration before oligarchic power consolidates; procurement and governance systems that reward learning rather than cost compression; and work organizations that enable collective capability formation. Above all, it requires institutions that lengthen temporality – interrupting capitalism's dominant tendencies long enough for labor to transform itself. Democracy depends not on markets as such, but on the plurality of capitals and on sustained class struggle to limit capitalism's brutalizing forces.

Chapter 15.
What Must Change: Conceptual, Institutional, Organizational, and Democratic Reforms – Systemic Summery

National and international class struggle must be oriented to restoring structural antitrust, countervailing power, and the architecture of pluralism within the bourgeois democracy.

Local class struggle at firm level must be directed towards reorienting production and competition toward capability development rather than price discipline.

16. Transition Reframed: Learning, Temporality, and the Limits of Emancipation

16.1 Transition as a temporally extended process

Marx could not fully finish his project to understand the capitalist economy and hence was neither able to build the foundation of a 'Marxist' political theory. In my doctoral dissertation (1980) I held that socialism must be built on reform ***and*** revolution.

Until the transcendence is achieved, this struggle has clear limits, by the essential elements of the capitalist economy. Capital will until then, again and again enforce its complete subsumption of the work process.

Transition is not a moment, not a rupture alone, and not a purely political act. It is a temporally extended process of institutionally protected learning within and against capitalism.

The argument developed here draws on classical political economy, evolutionary theory of the firm, institutional political economy, and historical analyses of class struggle.

Marx and Engels' vision of a new and better society was hijacked by demagogues with no interest whatsoever in liberating the working class. They used the vision as new speak for quite another agenda. It is time to take the vision back and fight for the changes necessary already within capitalism to realize the vision.

This book has sought to reclaim Marx's project from both economism and authoritarian misappropriation. Marx demonstrated that capitalism contains powerful systemic tendencies toward concentration and centralization of capital. Left unchecked, these tendencies lead not to freedom, but to the rule of an oligarchic class.

Much of twentieth-century Marxism interpreted these tendencies mechanically, as forces to be accelerated rather than resisted. On that reading, concentration itself was taken as a precondition of socialism. The historical outcome of this interpretation is well known: not workers' self-rule, but authoritarian domination exercised in their name.

Marx's analysis, however, was never a doctrine of inevitability. Capitalism's dominant tendencies operate through competition—but competition itself is not uniform. Alongside price-based competition, which drives concentration and abstraction, capitalism periodically generates value-based forms of competition that depend on learning, differentiation, and human capability. These counter-tendencies are structurally fragile and historically temporary, but they are real.

Capitalism's dominant tendency toward price-based competition and concentration is systemic, but not temporally continuous. Class struggle operates by mediating, suspending, and redirecting this tendency through institutions that stabilize value-based competition. Only during such periods can workers accumulate the knowledge required to govern production. The overcoming of capitalism therefore presupposes not the acceleration of its inner logic, but its interruption long enough to transform the capacities of labor itself.

- Class struggle as mediation: suspending, redirecting, stabilizing learning regimes
- Transition as prolonged interruption of price discipline long enough to transform labor's capacities

16.2 Reform – revolution revisited

This figure conceptualizes socialist transition as a process in which workers gain influence over parts of the producing and market-relating functions of capital, prior to any transformation of ownership.

Reform and revolution are treated not as opposites, but as different moments within a continuous process of class struggle inside capitalism.

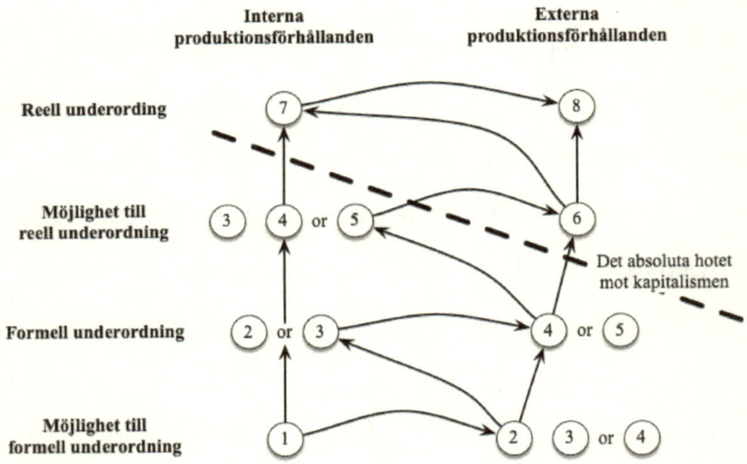

Figure 25. Limits of workers' empowerment during capitalism (after Philipson, 1980: 161 and 167)

Seen retrospectively, the reform – revolution figure anticipated the direction of transition correctly and rejected both reformist passivity and Leninist substitution, but lacked a theory of temporality, capability formation, and functional competition – elements that only became analytically visible with later transformations of the capitalist mode of production.

What was missing in 1980 was an analysis of the organizational and competitive mechanisms through which capital could be compelled to concede influence. The present book provides that missing explanation. In contemporary capitalism, production is organized through functionally differentiated product architectures and value chains, in which competition is not uniform but function specific. Some functions are governed primarily by price-base competition, while others depend on value-based competition rooted in learning, tacit knowledge, coordination, and reliability.

Where such collective worker capabilities, are a material necessity value creation, capital cannot sustain competitive advantage without cooperation from labor. Under these conditions, workers' knowledge becomes a material bargaining resource, making influence over producing and market-relating functions possible within capitalism. Class struggle thus operates not only through wages or political institutions, but through the gradual acquisition and institutionalization of functional influence over value creation. This clarifies how the process sketched abstractly in the original figure can, under specific historical conditions, become real and durable.

16.3 Capability, substitution, and the failure of emancipation

What I propose in this book is a theory of transition grounded in learning, temporality, and mediated class struggle.

Equally central to Marx's project was the claim that the emancipation of the working class must be the work of the working class itself. Emancipation therefore presupposes the development of material capabilities: knowledge of production, coordination, and collective decision-making. Without these capabilities, liberation can only take the form of substitution – rule over workers rather than rule by them.

The Korsnäs case demonstrates that such capability development is possible within capitalism, when class struggle extends beyond wages and conditions into the organization of production and learning itself. These gains are never secure. They require institutional protection and continuous struggle against capitalism's dominant tendencies. But without such periods of suspended price discipline, the capacities necessary for democratic control of production cannot emerge.

The lesson is therefore neither reformist nor insurrectionary in the conventional sense. Capitalism cannot be overcome by accelerating its inner logic, nor by political seizure alone. It can only be transcended by interrupting its dominant tendencies long enough for labor to transform itself. Without that transformation, emancipation remains a promise that repeatedly turns into its opposite.

Systemic Summary —
Capitalism, Class Struggle, and Transition

The Capitalism's dominant tendencies toward concentration and oligarchy are systemic but historically mediated.

Marx's insight that the emancipation of the working class must be its own work presupposes the development of collective capabilities grounded in learning, practice, and scientific knowledge.

Transition therefore depends not only on interrupting price-based competition, but on sustaining value-based competition long enough for workers to build the capacities required to subsume the functions of capital.

Where such capability formation is absent, emancipation is replaced by command, and liberation becomes domination in a new language.

Epilogue: Crisis, war, and the uncertain future of capitalism

Capitalism is going through one of its most profound cyclical crises. The profit quote has diminished since the 1960s (Basu *et al.*, 2022). In such a crisis the importance of the analysis of different strata of the capitalist class becomes paramount. The capitalists in department I (raw material extraction and refinement and the production of means of production) has the possibility to pursue a different strategy, by transforming itself to war industry. This is exactly what is happening now; imperialist competition is rising with more difficulties to uphold global supply chains. It is still too early to speculate about how this will transform capitalism.

Sarah Philipson is a Swedish Marxist scholar whose work spans academia, industry, and state administration.

Between 1969 and 1981, she worked as a university lecturer, metal worker, home-care worker, reader for recorded books for the blind, head of section at the Swedish Ministry of Industry, and researcher at the Royal Institute of Technology in Stockholm. In 1980, she was awarded a Ph.D. in Business Administration from Linköping University, Sweden.

From 1981 until 2003, she worked as a management consultant and senior executive in Scandinavian industry. She then returned to academia and became Associate Professor. Since her retirement in 2016, she has been affiliated with Linnaeus University and the University of Gävle, Sweden.

She has one son and two granddaughters.

References

Adner, R. (2017), Ecosystem as structure: An actionable construct for strategy, *Journal of Management*, 43(1), 39-58.

Alexander (1964). *Notes on the Synthesis of Form*. Harvard University Press, Cambridge,

Allen, B. (2005). Alexander Shliapnikov and the Origins of the Workers' Opposition, March 1919-April 1920. J*ahrbücher für Geschichte Osteuropas*, 1-24.

Alvesson, M., & Sandberg, J. (2011). Generating research questions through problematization. *Academy of Management Review*, 36(2), 247-271.

Alternet (2017-05-09) Documents Reveal a Powerful, Secretive Foundation's Blueprint for Spreading Right-Wing Ideology, State by State. 2017-05-07. Retrieved from: https://www.alternet.org/right-wing/bradley-foundation-far-right-agenda?akid=15537.2659157.MXl0Pu&rd=1&src=newsletter1076701&t=6 https://www.alternet.org/right-wing/bradley-foundation-far-right-agenda?akid=15537.2659157.MXl0Pu&rd=1&src=newsletter1076701&t=6

Amin, A., & Roberts, J. (2008). Knowing in action: Beyond communities of practice. Research Policy, 37(2), 353-369.

Asymco (2013-06-28). Retrieved from: http://www.asymco.com/2011/07/29/apple-captured-two-thirds-of-available-mobile-phone-profits-in-q2/ (with permission).

Avison, D.E., Lau, F., Myers, M.D., & Nielsen, P.A. (1999). Action research. *Communications of the ACM*, 42(1), 94-97.

Bach, D., Newman, A., & Weber, S. (2005). China's impact on the global economy: From China price to China standard. *IE Working Paper WP05/31*. Madrid, ES: IE Publishing.

Baran, P.A., & Sweezy, P.M. (1970) *Monopoly Capital*, Harmondsworth: Pelican.

Basu, D., Huato, J., Jauregui, J.L., & Wasner, E. (2022) World Profit Rates, 1960-2019, *Review of Political Economy*, 1-16. DOI: 10.1080/09538259.2022.2140007

BBC (2017-05-04) Apple 'failing to protect Chinese factory workers', 2014, Retrieved from: http://www.bbc.com/news/business-30532463

Berger, P., & Luckmann, T. (1967). *The social construction of reality*. New York, NY: Anchor

Bettelheim, C., Charriere J., & Marchisio H. (1968) *La construction du socialisme en Chine*, Maspero: Paris.

Bettelheim, C. (1970a) *Ökonomischer Kalkül und Eigentumsformen*, Wagenbach: Berlin.

Bettelheim, C. (1970b) *Övergången till den socialistiska ekonomin*, Partisan: Halmstad.

Bettelheim, C. (1970c) *La transition vers l'économie socialiste*, Maspero: Paris.

Bettelheim, C. (1970d) *Planification & Croissance Accélérée*, Paris: Maspero.

Bettelheim, C. (1971a) *L'économie allemande sous le nazisme - Un aspect de la décadence du capitalisme - Tome II*, Paris: Maspero.

Bettelheim, C. (1971b) *Socialism och Ekonomisk Planering*, Mölndal, Coeckelberg.

Bettelheim, C. (1972) *Planeringsdebatten på Kuba: värdelag, planering, medvetenhet*, Halmstad: Rabén & Sjögren.

Bettelheim, C. (1973) *Kulturrevolution och industriell organisering i Kina*, Partisan: Kristianstad.

Bettelheim, C. (1976), *Economic Calculation and Forms of Property*, Routledge and Kegan Paul: London.

Blomqvist, H. (2014) Lost Worlds of Labour: Paul Olberg, the Jewish Labour Bund, and Menshevik Socialism, in Göta, N. (Ed.), *The Sea of Identities: A Century of Baltic and East European Experiences with Nationality, Class, and Gender*, Huddinge: Södertörn University.

Boland Jr, R. J., & Tenkasi, R. V. (1995). Perspective making and perspective taking in communities of knowing. *Organization Science*, 6(4), 350-372.

Borkin, J. (1980) *Hitler & IG Farben*, Stockholm: Tiden.

Borrus, M., & Zysman, J. (1997). Globalization with borders: The rise of Wintelism as the future of industrial competition. *Industry and Innovation*, 42: 141-166.

Borthick, A. F., Jones, D. R., & Wakai, S. (2003). Designing Learning experiences within learners' zones of proximal development (ZPDs): Enabling collaborative learning on-site and online. *Journal of Information Systems*, 17(1), 107-134.

Bourdieu, P. (1976). Le sens pratique, *Actes De La Recherche En Sciences Sociales*, 2(1), 43-86. doi: 10.3406/arss.1976.3383

Braverman, H. (1974). *Labor and Monopoly Capital: The Degradation of Work in the Twentieth Century*, New York: Monthly Review Press.

Brown, J. S., & Duguid, P. (1991). Organizational learning and communities-of-practice: Toward a unified view of working, learning, and innovation. *Organization Science*, 2(1), 40-57.

Chandler, A. D. (1962). *Strategy and structure*, MIT Press.

Chattopadhyay, P. (2003). Two Approaches to Socialist Revolution: Marx versus Lenin-Trotsky, 5-8, in *the Conference "The Work of Karl Marx and the Challenges of the 21st Century"* Havana, Cuba, May. Retrieved from: www. countdowninfo. net/ uploads/6/7/3/6/6736569/chattopadhyay_marx_vs_lenin_countd own.Doc.

Economic Policy Institute (2017-05-04) Apple's employees in China don't work 70 hours a week because they want to 2012.

Retrieved from: http://www.epi.org/blog/apple-china-working-conditions/

Clarke, S. (1990). New utopias for old: Fordist dreams and post-Fordist fantasies. *Capital & Class*, 14(3), 131-155.

Coram, B. T. (1989) Social Relations and Forces of Production: A Criticism of Cohen's Defense of Materialism, *Social Theory and Practice*, 15(2), 213-229, https://www.jstor.org/stable/23557067

Corry, L. (1992) Nicolas Bourbaki and the concept of mathematical structure, *Synthese*, 92, 315-348.

Courier International (2024-11-28), Derrière J. D. Vance, l'ombre du milliardaire Peter Thiel, Retrieved from: https://www.courrierinternational.com/article/etats-unis-derriere-j-d-vance-l-ombre-du-milliardaire-peter-thiel_224581

Dietzgen, J. (1973) *Das Weser der Menschligen Kopfarbeit and Andrée Schriften*, Luchterhand: Darmstadt.

Eisenhardt, K. M. (1989) Agency Theory: An Assessment and Review, *Academy of Management Review*, 14(1), 57-74.

Elliott, J. E. (1980). Marx and Schumpeter on capitalism's creative destruction: A comparative restatement. *The Quarterly Journal of Economics*, 95(1), 45-68.

Estes, R.J., & Weine, N.A. (2002), *The Commercial Sexual Exploitation of Children in the U. S., Canada and Mexico*, University of Pennsylvania, School of Social Work, Center for the Study of Youth Policy: Philadelphia, PA.

Ferguson, E. S. (1992). *Engineering and the mind's eye*, Cambridge, MA: The MIT Press.

Foucault, M. (2008). *The birth of biopolitics: Lectures at the Collège de France, 1978-1979*, London: Palgrave Macmillan.

Freud, S. (1974). *Introductory lectures on psychoanalysis*, Harmondsworth, UK: Penguin

Glattfelder, J.B. (2010). *Ownership Networks and Corporate Control: Mapping Economic Power in a Globalized World*, Zürich: ETH Zürich.

Grachev, M., & Rakitsky, B. (2013). Historic horizons of Frederick Taylor's scientific management. *Journal of Management History*, 19(4), 512-527.

Gramsci, A. (1971) *Selections from the Prison Notebooks*, London: Lawrence and Wishart.

Granovetter, M. S. (1985) Economic action and social structure: the problem of embeddedness, *American Journal of Sociology*, 91(3), 481-510.

Guerin, D. (1939/1973) *Fascism and Big Business*, NY: Monad.

Hacker, J. S., & Pierson, P. (2010). *Winner-take-all politics*, NY: Simon & Schuster.

Hart, J. A., & Kim, S. (2002). Explaining the resurgence of U.S. competitiveness: The rise of Wintelism. *The Information Society*, 18(1), 1-12.

Herrenkohl, L. R., & Guerra, M. R. (1998). Participant structures, scientific discourse, and student engagement in fourth grade, *Cognition and Instruction*, 16(4), 431-473.

Herrenkohl, L. R., Palincsar, A. S., DeWater, L. S., & Kawasaki, K. (1999). Developing scientific communities in classrooms: A sociocognitive approach. *Journal of the Learning Sciences*, 8(3-4), 451-493.

Hirschman, D., & Berman, E. P. (2014). Do economists make policies? *Socio-Economic Review*, 12(4), 779-811.

Holbrook, M. B. (1982). Some further dimensions of psycholinguistics, imagery, and consumer response. *Advances in Consumer Research*, 9(1), 112-117.

International Labour Organization. (2015). W*orld employment and social outlook: Trends 2015*, Geneva: International Labour Office. https://www.ilo.org/global/research/global-reports/weso/2015/lang–en/index.htm

Jacoby, S. M. (1983). Union-management cooperation in the United States: Lessons from the 1920s. *Industrial and Labor Relations Review*, 37(1), 18-33.

John-Steiner, V., & Mahn, H. (1996). Sociocultural approaches to learning and development: A Vygotskian framework, *Educational Psychologist*, 31(3/4), 191-206.

Kaufmann, A. (1967) *Graphs, Dynamic Programming, and Finite Games*, Academic Press: New York.

Kelley, T. (2001). Prototyping is the shorthand of design, *Design Management Journal*, 12(3), 35-42.

Khan, L. (2019). The separation of powers in platform markets, *Columbia Law Review*, 119, 973-1092.

Kuhn, T.S. (1968) *The Structure of Scientific Revolutions*, University of Chicago Press: Chicago.

Kim, S. (2002). “Hardware" institutions for ‘software" technologies: The Japanese model of industrial development in the personal computer industry. *Journal of International and Area Studies*, 9(1), 17-36.

Kinginger, C. (2002). Defining the zone of proximal development in US foreign language education, *Applied Linguistics*, 23(2), 240-261.

Kjellström, E. (2019) *Outsourcing of Organizational Routines. Knowledge, Control, and Learning Aspects*, Lund Studies in Economics and Management No. 143. Lund University: Lund.

Kozulin, A., & Presseisen, B.Z. (1995). Mediated Learning Experience and Psychological Tools: Vygotsky's and Feuerstein's Perspectives in a Study of Student Learning, *Educational Psychologist*, 30(2), 67-75.

Lam, A. (2014). Tacit knowledge, embedded agency and learning: Local nodes and global networks. *Prometheus*, 32(1), 93-99.

Lave, J., & Wenger, E. (1991). *Situated learning: Legitimate peripheral participation,* Cambridge: Cambridge University Press.

Levykh, M. G. (2008). The affective establishment and maintenance of Vygotsky's zone of proximal development. *Educational Theory*, 58(1), 83-101.

Lindblom, C. E. (1977). Politics and markets. Basic Books.

Lindqvist, S. (1978), *Gräv där du står: hur man utforskar ett jobb*, Stockholm: Bonnier.

LO (2022-06-26) Medbestämmande [Co-determination]. retrieved from: https://www.lo.se/start/politiska_sakfragor/arbetsratt/lagarna/medbestammande

Lloyd, A. (2017) Ideology at Work: Reconsidering ideology, the labour process and workplace resistance, *International Journal of Sociology and Social Policy*, 37(5/6), 266-279.

LSE (2014-04-05), British mining companies' exploitation of Sierra Leone. Retrieved from: http://blogs.lse.ac.uk/africaatlse/2013/12/23/british-mining-companies-exploitation-of-sierra-leone/.

Luce, L. R., & Raiffa, H. (1957). *Games and Decisions: Introduction and Critical Survey*, Hoboken, NJ: Wiley.

Luxemburg, R. (1913/1963) *The Accumulation of Capital*, London: Routledge.

Lüthje, B. (2002). Electronics contract manufacturing: Global production and the international division of labor in the age of the Internet, *Industry and Innovation*, 9(3), 227–247.

MacRumors (2024-05-01) Profit Margin Tensions Souring Relationship Between Apple and Foxconn, Retrieved from: https://www.macrumors.com/2020/10/27/apple-foxconn-profit-margin-tensions/

Mahn, H., & John-Steiner, V. (2002). The gift of confidence: A Vygotskian view of emotions, 46-59, in G. Wells & G Claxton (Eds.), *Learning for life in the 21st century: Socio-cultural perspectives of future education*, Oxford, UK: Blackwell Publish.

Maier, C.S. (1970). Between Taylorism and technocracy: European ideologies and the vision of industrial productivity in the 1920s, *Journal of Contemporary History*, 5(2), 27-61.

Malthus, T. R. (1798/1970). *An Essay on the Principle of Population*, Harmondsworth: Penguin Books.

March, J. G. (1991). Exploration and exploitation. *Organization Science*, 2(1), 71-87.

Marx, K. (1962) Class struggles in France 1848 to 1850, in *Selected Works*, London: Lawrence & Wishart.

Marx, K. (1969a) *Resultate des unmittelbaren Produktionsprozesses*, Neue Kritik: Frankfurt.

Marx, K. (1969b) *Theories of surplus value, Volume 1*, Lawrence & Wishart: London.

Marx, K. (1969c) *Theories of Surplus Value, Volume II*, London: Lawrence and Wishart.

Marx, K. (1970a) *Capital, Volume I, The Process of Production of Capital*, International Publisher: New York.

Marx, K. (1970c) Critique of the Gotha program, in *Selected Works*, London: Lawrence & Wishart.

Marx, K. (1894/1970) *Capital, Volume III*, New York: International Publisher.

Marx, K. (1972b) *Civil war in France*, New York: Progress Publishers.

Marx K. (1979) The 18th Brumaire of Louis Bonaparte, in *Marx and Engels, Selected Works*, Englewood Cliffs: Lawrence and Wishart.

Marx, K. (1970) *Grundriße der Kritik der Politischen Ökonomie*, Frankfurt: Europeische Verlagsanstalt.

Marx, K. (1973) *Grundrisse*, Harmondsworth: Pelican.

Marx, K., & Engels, F. (1848) Manifesto of the Communist Party, 98-137, in Marx, K., & Engels, F. (1969) *Selected Works, Vol. One*, Progress Publishers: Moscow.

McGeever, B. (2017) Revolution and antisemitism: the Bolsheviks in 1917, *Patterns of Prejudice*, 5(3-4), 235-252, DOI: 10.1080/0031322X.2017.1351798

Mediapart (2023-01-07) En 2023, l'économie mondiale s'enfoncera dans sa crise structurelle, retrieved from: https://

www.mediapart.fr/journal/economie-et-social/070123/en-2023-l-economie-mondiale-s-enfoncera-dans-sa-crise-structurelle#:~:text=et%20social%20Analyse-,En%202023%2C%20l'économie%20mondiale%20s'enfoncera%20dans%20sa,d'une%20crise%20de%20régime.

Meyers, J. (2019). A Portrait of Transition: From the Bund to Bolshevism in the Russian Revolution. *Jewish Social Studies*, 24(2), 107-134.

Miller, R. W. (1981) Productive Forces and the Forces of Change: A Review of Gerald A. Cohen, Karl Marx's Theory of History: A Defense, *The Philosophical Review*, 90(1), 91-117, https://www.jstor.org/stable/2184374

Mintzberg H. (1979) *The Structuring of Organizations*, Englewood Cliffs: Prentice-Hall.

Nelson, R. R., & Winter, S. G. (1982). *An evolutionary theory of economic change*, Cambridge, MA: Harvard University Press.

Orwell, G (1949), *1984*, London: Secker & Warburg.

Orr, J. E. (1996). *Talking about machines: An ethnography of a modern job*, Ithaca, NY: Cornell University Press.

Palinscar, A. S., & Herrenkohl, R. L. (2002). Designing collaborative learning contexts. *Theory in Practice*, 41(1), 26-32.

Peña, D.S. (2014) The Six Essential Components of Sustainable Socialism: From Building the Productive Forces to Combating

Bourgeois Liberalization, *International Critical Thought*, 493), 267-288. DOI: 10.1080/21598282.2014.930987

Penrose, E. (1959/2009). *Theory of the Growth of the Firm*, Oxford: Oxford University Press.

Petras, J. (1983). Workers' Democracy: The Key to Defending the Revolution and Developing the Productive Forces: Response to Richard Harris, *Latin American Perspectives*, 10(1), 117-119.

Philipson, S. (1980) *Kapitalfunktioner och arbetarnas ställning: marxistisk analys av företag utifrån arbetarkollektivets intressen* [Capital functions and the position of the workers; Marxist analysis of companies from the interests of worker collective], Doctoral Dissertation, Linköping University, Linköping. LIBRIS-ID: 7638092 http://libris.kb.se/bib/7638092?vw=full

Philipson, S. (2016). Radical innovation of a business model. Competitiveness Review, 26(2). 132-146. http://doi.org/10.1108/CR-06-2015-0061

Philipson, S., & Philipson, J. (2016). From Budapest to Berlin – the role of reputation in the market economy. *International Journal of Entrepreneurship and Small Business*, 28(2/3), 310-322.

Philipson, S., Johansson, J., & Schley, D. (2016). Global Corporate Governance: The Maelstrom of Increased Complexity – Is It Possible to Learn to Ride the Dragon? *Journal of Business and Economics*, 7(3), 425-437. http://doi.org/DOI:10.15341/jbe(2155-7950)/03.07.2016/007

Philipson, S. (2016b) A framework for entrepreneurial learning in higher education, 124-162, in *Proceedings from Lärarlärdom: Conference on higher education*, Linnaeus University, http://doi.org/10.15626/lld.201507

Philipson, S. (2019) The difficulty with which tacit knowing is transformed into explicit knowledge, *World Review of Entrepreneurship, Management and Sustainable Development*, 15(3), 346-359.

Philipson, S. (2020a) Sources of innovation: Consequences for knowledge production and transfer, *Journal of Innovation & Knowledge*, 5(1), 50-58.

Philipson, S. (2020b). Consumers and enterprises as actors on the market, *Harvard Deusto Business Research*, 9(2), 168-180. https://doi.org/10.48132/hdbr.302

Philipson, S. (2021). Cost-Structure and the Volatility of Capitalism, *Harvard Deusto Business Research*, 10(1), 146-156. https://doi.org/10.48132/hdbr.340.

Philipson, S. (2022a). Value – The "Atom" of the Economy. *Journal of Applied Business and Economics*, 24(5), 170-180.

Philipson, S. (2022b). The end of the present mode of production – a new Kondratieff wave? – new directions for research?

International *Journal of Innovation and Technology Management*, 19(3), 2240002, https://doi.org/10.1142/S0219877022400028

Philipson, S., & Kjellström, E, (2020) When objects are talking: How tacit knowing becomes explicit knowledge, *Journal of Small Business Strategy*, 30(1), 68-82.

Pirani, S. (2004) The Moscow workers' movement in 1921 and the role of non-partyism, *Europe-Asia Studies*, 56(1), 143-160, DOI: 10.1080/0966813032000161473

Pirani, S. (2008) Introduction, 1-18, in Pirani, S. (2008) *The Russian revolution in retreat, 1920–24: Soviet workers and the new communist elite*, Milton Park, UK: Routledge.

Pistor, K. (2019). *The code of capital*, Princeton University Press.

Polanyi, K. (1944). The great transformation. Beacon Press.

Polanyi, M. (1961). The logic of tacit inference. *Philosophy*, 41(155), 1-18.

Polanyi, M. (1962). Tacit knowing: Its bearing on some problems of philosophy. *Reviews of Modern Physics*, 34(4), 601-616.

Polanyi, M. (1968). Logic and psychology, *American Psychologist*, 23(1), 27-43.

Poulantzas, N. (1970) *Politisk Makt och Sociala Klasser*, Mölndal: Coeckelberg.

Poulantzas, N. (1978) *Classes in Contemporary Capitalism*, London: Verso.

Pool, J., & Pool, S. (1980) *Who Financed Hitler. The Secret Funding of Hitler's Rise to Power 1919-1933*, London: Futura.

Ravallion, M., & Wodon, Q. (2000), Does Child-labour displace Schooling? Evidence on Behavioural Response to an Enrollment Subsidy, *The Economic Journal*, 110, C158-C175.

Ricardo, D. (1817/1971). *On the Principles of Political Economy and Taxation*, Harmondsworth: Penguin Books.

Rigby, T. H. (1976). Soviet communist party membership under Brezhnev, *Soviet Studies*, 28(3), 317-337.

Rubin, A. I. (1973/1990) Productive Labour, chapter 19, in Rubin, A.I. *Essays on Marx's Theory of Value*, Dehli: Aakar Books.

Sandberg, A. (1994). "Volvoism" at the End of the Road? *Studies in Political Economy*, 45(1), 170–182.

SCB (2017-07-09) Företag och anställda (FDB) efter näringsgren SNI 2007, storleksklass, tabellinnehåll år 2011, https://www.statistikdatabasen.scb.se/pxweb/sv/ssd/START__NV__NV0101/FDBR07/

Schalow, T. (2013). Shared knowledge: Eliminating the "ba", 594, in B. Janiũnaité, A. Pundziene, & M. Petraite (Eds.), *ECKM 2013 14th European conference on knowledge management*, Reading, UK: Academic Conferences International Limited.

Schumpeter, J. A. (1942). *Capitalism, Socialism and Democracy*, New York: Harper and Brothers.

Schumpeter, J. A. (1947). The Creative Response in Economic History. *The Journal of Economic History*, 7(2), 149-159.

Shandro, A. (1997/1998) Karl Kautsky: On the Relation of Theory and Practice, *Science & Society*, 61(4), 474-501.

Simon, H. A. (1976). *Administrative Behavior: A Study of Decision-Making Processes in Administrative Organization*, 3rd ed., New York: Free Press.

Smith, A. (1776/1982). *The Wealth of Nations*, London: Penguin.

Smith, S. (2007). Revolution and Counterrevolution: Class Struggle in a Moscow Metal Factory, *Historical Materialism*, 15(4), 167-185. doi: https://doi.org/10.1163/156920607X245887

Star, S. L. (2010). This is not a boundary object: Reflections on the origin of a concept, *Science, Technology & Human Values*, 35(5), 601-617. https://doi.org/10.1177/016224391037762

Strategic Analytics (2016-11-25). Retrieved from: https://www.strategyanalytics.com

Streeck, W. (2011). The crises of democratic capitalism, *New Left Review*, 71, 5-29.

Sunesson, S. (1974) *Politik och organisation*, Lund: Arkiv.

Sutton, J. (1991). *Sunk costs and market structure*, MIT Press.

Sutton, J. (1998). *Technology and market structure*, MIT Press.

Söderpalm, S. Å. (1970) *Wallenberg och Branting*, Lund: Gleerups.

Söderpalm, S. Å. (1976) *Direktörsklubben. Storindustri i svensk politik under 1930- och 40-talen*, Stockholm: Zenit/Rabén & Sjögren.

Tan, Z. A. (2002). Product cycle, Wintelism, and cross-national production networks (CPN) for developing countries – China's telecom manufacturing industry as a case. *Info*, 4(3), 57-65.

Teece, D. J., Pisano, G., & Shuen, A. (1997). Dynamic capabilities and strategic management. *Strategic Management Journal*, 18(7), 509-533.

The Guardian (2017-12-02). The great British Brexit robbery: how our democracy was hijacked, 2017.05.-07 Retrieved from: https://www.theguardian.com/technology/2017/may/07/the-great-british-brexit-robbery-hijacked-democracy

The Guardian (2022-01-11) Why is so little known about the 1930s coup attempt against FDR?, retrieved from: https://www.theguardian.com/commentisfree/2022/jan/11/trump-fdr-roosevelt-coup-attempt-1930s

Therborn, G. (1971) *Klasser och ekonomiska system*, Lund: Cavefors.

Therborn, G. (1972) Om klasserna i Sverige 1930-1970, *Zenit* 17(28), 4-230.

Thompson, J. D. (1967) *Organizations in Action*, McGraw-Hill: New York.

Tobias, H.G. (1965). The Bund and the First Congress of the RSDWP: An Addendum, *The Russian Review*, 24(4), 393-406.

Tsai, J., & Wright, J. (2014). *Standard setting, intellectual property rights, and the role of antitrust in regulating incomplete contracts. Working paper series no. 15002*, Hoover institution working group on intellectual property, innovation, and prosperity. CA: Stanford University.

Ulrich, K. (1995), The role of product architecture in the manufacturing firm, *Research Policy*, 24(3), 419-440.

Unger, A. L. (1977). Soviet communist party membership under Brezhnev: A comment, *Soviet Studies*, 29(2), 306-316.

Van Der Lugt, R. (2005). How sketching can affect the idea generation process in design group meetings. *Design Studies*, 26(2), 101-122.

Vidal, M. (2019). Contradictions of the labour process, worker empowerment and capitalist inefficiency, *Historical Materialism*, 28(2), 170-204.

Voit, S., Tkachenko, V., & Oleshkevich, I. (2018). Intellectual potential as a means of reproduction and renewal of the unity of productive forces and industrial relations, *Economics, Management and Sustainability*, 3(1), 34-43.

Von Hippel, E. (1988). *The Sources of Innovation*, New York: Oxford University Press.

Von Hippel, E. (1990) Task Partitioning: An Innovation Process Variable, *Research Policy*, 19(5), 407-418.

Von Neumann, J., & Morgenstern, O. (1944/2007). *Theory of Games and Economic Behavior*, Princeton, NJ: Princeton University Press.

Vygotsky, L. S. (1970). *Thought and language*, Cambridge, MA: MIT.

Vygotsky, L. S. (1987). *The collected works of L. S. Vygotsky: Problems of general psychology, including the volume thinking and speech. (Vol. 1)*, R. W. Reiber & A. S. Carton (Eds.). NY: Springer Science & Business Media LCC.

Vygotsky, L. S. (1993). *The collected works of L. S. Vygotsky: The fundamentals of defectology (abnormal psychology and learning disabilities) (Vol. 2)*, R. W. Reiber & A. S. Carton (Eds.). New York, NY: Springer Science & Business Media LCC.

Vygotsky, L. (1994). Imagination and creativity of the adolescent, 266-288, in R. van der Veer, & J. Valsiner (Eds.), *The Vygotsky reader*, Oxford, UK: Blackwell.

Vygotsky, L. S. (1997a). *The collected works of L. S. Vygotsky: Problems of the theory and history of psychology (Vol. 3)*, R. W. Reiber & J. Wollock (Eds.). New York, NY: Springer Science & Business Media LCC.

Vygotsky, L. S. (1997b). *The collected works of L. S. Vygotsky: The history of the development of higher mental functions (Vol.4)*,

R. W. Rieber (Ed.). New York, NY: Springer Science & Business Media LCC.

Vygotsky, L. S. (1998). *The collected works of L. S. Vygotsky: Child psychology (Vol. 5)*, R. W. Rieber (Ed.). New York, NY: Springer Science & Business Media LCC.

Vygotsky, L. S. (1999). *The collected works of L. S. Vygotsky: Scientific legacy. (Vol. 6)*, R. W. Rieber (Ed.). New York, NY: Springer Science & Business Media LCC.

Weick, K. E., & Roberts, K. H. (1993). Collective mind in organizations: Heedful interrelating on flight decks, *Administrative Science Quarterly*, 38(3), 357-381.

Wenger, E. (1998). *Communities of practice: Learning, meaning, and identity*, Cambridge, UK: Cambridge University Press.

Wenger, E. (2000). Communities of practice and social learning systems. *Organization*, 7(2), 225-246.

Wenger, E. C., & Snyder, W. M. (2000). Communities of practice: The organizational frontier, *Harvard Business Review*, 78(1), 139-145.

Wertheimer, M., Brett, M. D., King, M. A., Peckler, S. R., & Schaef, R. W. (1992). Carl Ljung and Max Wertheimer on a priority issue. *Journal of the History of the Behavioral Sciences*, 28(1), 45-46.

Wikipedia (2021-02-01) Moore's law, retrieved from: *https://commons.wikimedia.org/wiki/File:Moore%27s Law Transistor Count 1970-2020.png.*

Wikipedia (2026-01-11) Armed Forces Movement, *https://en.wikipedia.org/wiki/Armed_Forces_Movement?wprov=sfti1*

Williamson, O. E. (1973). Markets and hierarchies: some elementary considerations, *The American Economic Review*, 63(2), 316-325.

Williamson, O. E. (1992) Markets, hierarchies, and the modern corporation, *Journal of Economic Behaviour and Organization*, 17(3), 335-352.

Winters, J. A. (2011). *Oligarchy*. Cambridge University Press.

Wolfson, T., & Funke, P. (2018). The History of all Hitherto Existing Society: Class Struggle and the Current Wave of Resistance, *tripleC: Communication, Capitalism & Critique, Open Access Journal for a Global Sustainable Information Society,* 16(2), 577-587.

Wren, D. A., & Bedeian, A. G. (2004). The Taylorization of Lenin: rhetoric or reality? *International Journal of Social Economics*, 31(3), 287-299.

York, R., Rosa, E.A., & Dietz, T. (2003) Footprints on the Earth: The Environmental Consequences of Modernity, *American Sociological Review*, 68(2), 279-300.

Zuboff, S. (2019). *The age of surveillance capitalism: The Fight for a Human Future at the New Frontier of Power*, New York: Public Affairs (The Hatchett Group). https://www.publicaffairsbooks.com/titles/shoshana-zuboff/the-age-of-surveillance-capitalism/9781610395694/

Zysman, J., & Schwartz, A. (Eds.). (1998). *Enlarging Europe: The Industrial Foundations of a New Political Reality*, Berkeley, CA: UC Berkeley GAIA Research Series 99.

Ödman, H. (1985) *På Jakt Efter Socialismens Historiska Nödvändighet - En Kritik av Rosa Luxemburgs Teori om Kapitalackumulationen*, Göteborg :Göteborgs Universitet.

Øversveen, E. (2022). Capitalism and alienation: Towards a Marxist theory of alienation for the 21st century. *European Journal of Social Theory*, 25(3), 440-457.

Interviews

Klas Eklund (2023-01-18), former assistant to the social democratic minister of finances, former chief economist of Skandinaviska Enskilda Banken; the biggest Swedish bank.

Joe Gibbs (2020-11-04), former revolutionary in British Guayana, editor of the Korsnäs labor union paper, Karskäringen.

Åke Lamm (2020-01-15; 2020-03-04), former board member and then former chairman of the labor union at Korsnäs

Bengt Westerberg (2023-04-24), former secretary of state at the ministry of industry, former secretary of state at the ministry of budget, former minister of social affairs, deputy prime minister, former chairman of the Folkpartiet, the liberal people's party.

Ulf Westin (2020-10-02; 2020-11-23), former board member and then chair of the Korsnäs labor union.

Marx Right Side Up

Capitalism, Class Struggle, and the Recovery of Marx's Project

For more than a century, Marx's analysis of capitalism has been misread in two opposing ways: as economic determinism or as a justification for authoritarian rule. Both claim fidelity to Marx—and both miss his central insight.

Marx Right Side Up reconstructs Marx's project by returning to what has been most consistently neglected: class struggle as a historical process of learning, capability formation, and mediated transition. Drawing on political economy, organization theory, and an empirical case from Swedish industry, Sarah Philipson shows how capitalism's dominant tendency toward price-based competition and concentration can be interrupted through value-based competition, institutional mediation, and collective worker learning.

The book challenges three entrenched assumptions: that capitalism mechanically produces its own transcendence; that ownership is the primary lever of socialist transition; and that workers' emancipation can be delivered by parties, states, or elites acting in their name.

Neither a call for acceleration nor a defense of reformist accommodation, Marx Right Side Up argues that capitalism can only be overcome by suspending its dominant competitive logic long enough for labor to transform itself. Without that transformation, liberation becomes substitution—and freedom turns into rule over workers rather than rule by them.

www.ingramcontent.com/pod-product-compliance
Lightning Source LLC
LaVergne TN
LVHW100727061126
851857LV00011B/421
9789153179733